SECRET FORT LAUDERDALE

A Guide to the Weird, Wonderful, and Obscure

Christiana Lilly

Reedy Press
PO Box 5131
St. Louis, MO 63139
reedypress.com

Library of Congress Control Number: 2025936464
ISBN: 9781681066134

Design by Jill Halpin

Unless otherwise indicated, all photos are courtesy of the author or in the public domain.

Cover photos: *Top left* courtesy Broward County Public Library, *top right* courtesy City of Fort Lauderdale, *bottom left* courtesy Christiana Lilly, *bottom right* courtesy Downtown Photo.

Printed in the United States of America
25 26 27 28 29   5 4 3 2 1

To my parents, who fostered my sense of curiosity.

Photo courtesy of City of Pompano Beach

CONTENTS

Photo courtesy of T.J. Hunt Photography

ACKNOWLEDGMENTS

Writing this book meant looking up at buildings, reading plaques, living on Newspapers.com, and searching for the evidence behind local folklore and legends.

But it was the people of Greater Fort Lauderdale who guided me in writing this collection of stories, because that's what this is. Thank you to the people who entertained my questions as I prodded them for details while standing at the check-out counter or sitting outside on a lawn chair.

Thank you also to the cultural institutions and businesses that gave their time with interviews or a tour of their spaces, including the Old Dillard Museum, History Fort Lauderdale, Old Florida Book Shop, the Hillsboro Lighthouse, Christmas Palace, the African-American Research Library and Cultural Center, the Parker, Revolution Live, and many, *many* more.

Most of all, thank you to anyone who ever asked me, "Did you know . . . ?"

Photo courtesy of Seminole Tribune

INTRODUCTION

One of my favorite phrases, perhaps to the chagrin of people around me, is "Did you know . . . ?"

Did you know the first woman to get her concealed-carry license in Broward County was an archaeologist? Did you know this concert venue used to be a slaughterhouse? And did you know that there's a python-hunting competition every year? Did you know school was canceled when it snowed in the '70s?

I live for trivia and little-known facts, uncovering nuggets of information, and those are exactly what you'll find in *Secret Fort Lauderdale*. Not just hidden gems, but gems hidden in plain sight. A sign you've probably driven past countless times, a cemetery that's been long forgotten, papers tucked away in storage at the library, statues that have blended into the background, or pieces of Fort Lauderdale that no longer exist (but certainly left their mark). Some of it is humorous, a part of the Florida Man lore that haunts our weird and wonderful state. Other tales will make you cock your head and ask, "Really?" And then there are the stories you'll wish you had known sooner, and wonder why they aren't a part of the greater storytelling narrative of our community.

That's because every story has a light and dark side. I discovered that while exploring Fort Lauderdale and researching the stories behind the stories. It made me more curious about the place where we live.

After reading this, I hope you'll feel the same.

ONE GIANT LEAP FOR MANKIND

Where can you find a moon rock?

The moon is about 238,855 miles from earth, but you don't have to travel nearly that far to get up close and personal with a piece of it.

At the Broward County Main Library in Fort Lauderdale, a moon rock has been on permanent display—the first (and possibly only!) library in America to have the honor.

MOON ROCK

WHAT: A moon rock donated by an astronaut's wife

WHERE: Main Library, 100 S Andrews Ave., 6th floor, Fort Lauderdale

COST: Free to enter

PRO TIP: Check out the storefront art space on the first floor, where rotating resident artists work on their next pieces.

The rock was donated to the library by Susan Eisele Black, the wife of the late Command Module Pilot Donn F. Eisele. As a member of the Apollo 7 crew, he spent nearly 11 days in October 1968 orbiting the earth alongside Commander Walter M. Schirra, Jr. and Lunar Module Pilot R. Walter Cunningham. It was the first successful three-man space mission of its kind, and because of the trio's findings, NASA was able to send Apollo 8 to orbit the moon two months later.

For his service, Donn and other Apollo astronauts who went on missions from 1968 to 1972 were given pieces of the

---

The moon rock display also includes a newspaper with the Apollo 7 launch on the front page, as well as historic toys like an astronaut Barbie from 1965.

Top: *Command Module Pilot Donn F. Eisele was given the moon rock for his participation in the Apollo 7 mission. Courtesy Broward County Public Library*

Left: *A small piece of the moon is open to all at the Broward County Public Library.*

842 pounds of moon rock that had been collected by NASA, as a part of its Ambassador of Exploration Award Program.

The Eiseles were residents of Fort Lauderdale, and as a longtime member of the Broward Public Library Foundation, Susan generously donated the moon rock to the library so anyone could enjoy it. To this day, visitors to the library can get one step closer to being an astronaut by visiting the display.

DESEGREGATING THE BEACHES

When did the beaches become open for all?

Fort Lauderdale's beaches are a draw for tourists and locals alike, a place to soak up the sun, go snorkeling, or cool off in the water. But once upon a time the beaches were not open to just anyone looking to enjoy a day at the shore.

While walking down the sidewalk that runs along the beach, it's easy to pass a black-and-white plaque at the intersection of Las Olas Boulevard. But the historic marker is worth a stop to read. It commemorates the historic wade-ins during the summer of 1961, when black protesters took to the beach in an effort to desegregate the beaches. Starting on the Fourth of July, activists Eula Johnson and Dr. Von D. Mizell led black residents to take a dip in the Atlantic Ocean; some protests had as many as 200 swimmers.

The fight wasn't a one-and-done deal, though. The city of Fort Lauderdale struck back, suing the two and the NAACP. The lawsuits ultimately failed, leading to the desegregation of the city's beaches. The activists' legacy is marked with the plaque, and in 2016 a park was renamed after the two heroes; it's now the Dr. Von D. Mizell–Eula Johnson State Park in Hollywood. This location was also significant because it was a designated black beach since 1954, but local leadership never followed up on their promise to build roads to make

---

Dr. Von D. Mizell was the second black doctor in Fort Lauderdale and helped found Provident Hospital, a medical facility for black patients during a time of segregation.

Top: *A white police officer tells black protesters to leave Fort Lauderdale Beach. Courtesy History Fort Lauderdale*

Bottom: *A marker commemorates the wade-ins of 1961.*

WADE-INS OF 1961

WHAT: A plaque commemorating the wade-ins

WHERE: Across the street from 241 S Fort Lauderdale Beach Blvd., Fort Lauderdale

COST: Free to enter

PRO TIP: Use the Elbo Room bar as a landmark, then cross the street to find the sign.

it accessible to bathers. This meant that black beachgoers had to travel to neighboring counties to enjoy a day at the beach.

Now, though, the beach is open to all—and a small plaque at the beach makes sure we never forget it.

SWING LIFE AWAY

How does a bridge cost someone an election?

There are a few good excuses for when you're running late in Fort Lauderdale, and one is that you got stuck at the bridge. There are several of them here, stopping traffic to raise up and let towering yachts cross. But there's only one swing bridge in town, and it's one of the last in the entire state.

THE SNOW-REED SWING BRIDGE

WHAT: Fort Lauderdale's last swing bridge

WHERE: Intersection of Palm Avenue and the New River in Fort Lauderdale

COST: Free to enter

PRO TIP: Pedestrians are also able to cross the bridge, with a dedicated walk on both sides.

The Snow-Reed Swing Bridge on 11th Street connects the historic Sailboat Bend and Riverside Park neighborhoods. While most bridges separate at the middle and raise up to allow boats to cross, this one is an engineering marvel in that it swings in a circle, letting boats pass and then allowing cars to continue on their journey.

It was completed in 1925, replacing a wooden bridge, and was named after the two mayors whose terms overlapped the time during which the bridge was built: E.G. Snow and Will J. Reed. When it first opened, the bridge had to be turned manually by a bridge tender. A gasoline motor was installed five years later, and by the 1950s an electric motor was in the works. It was installed in 1954, and

---

The Snow-Reed Swing Bridge is considered a Broward Cultural Heritage Landmark, as indicated by a plaque designed by local artist Alicia Bellini-Sobchak.

The Snow-Reed Swing Bridge is one of the last of its kind in Florida.

mayoral candidate Mel Carlisle took credit for it during his 1955 campaign. The problem? It wasn't operational yet! It's said that this mishap cost him the election.

HANDLE WITH CARE

Do mailmen need shoes?

We need reminders in Greater Fort Lauderdale to wear shoes before entering an establishment, and can locals be blamed when there are miles of beach? Well, once upon a time, the federal employees who brought us our mail opted to do the job without shoes.

THE BAREFOOT MAILMAN

WHAT: A statue commemorating the Barefoot Mailmen

WHERE: 1212 Hillsboro Mile, Hillsboro Beach

COST: Free to enter

PRO TIP: A matching Barefoot Mailman statue is next to the Hillsboro Inlet Lighthouse, an area the mailmen would pass through.

Known as the Barefoot Mailmen, the 15 recorded mail carriers from 1885 to 1892 would walk 68 miles round trip to deliver mail to residents, a journey that took six days and was done every day of the week except Sunday. Around their necks they would carry their shoes laced together (try walking in the sand in boots). At that time, the US mail route only went as far south as Palm Beach County, meaning that those living in Greater Fort Lauderdale were dependent on these brave men to keep them connected to family and friends.

The Barefoot Mailman route was started by Edwin Ruthven Bradley and his son, Louie, who contracted with the government and brought on other mail carriers. It was

---

Thanks to the salt air and humidity in South Florida, the bronze Barefoot Mailman statues have turned green, not unlike the Statue of Liberty.

The statue honoring the legend of the Barefoot Mailman sits outside of Hillsboro Beach Town Hall.

a dangerous job, with the mailmen going up against alligators, rough currents, and loneliness. Sadly, one of the men, James "Ed" Hamilton, went missing and was never found—it's believed that he drowned while trying to cross the Hillsboro Inlet.

The Barefoot Mailman restaurant in Hillsboro Beach had a bronze statue of a mailman mid stride, and it was preserved after the restaurant burned down in 1988. In 1999, the statue was relocated to the front of Hillsboro Beach Town Hall and dedicated in honor of the town's 60th anniversary.

And yes, there is a USPS mailbox just steps away.

COLLEGIATE HEADQUARTERS

Where was Spring Break invented?

Fort Lauderdale Beach remains a popular spring break destination, with students from around the country descending upon the sandy stretch of beach to party their worries away. A bar that has seen it all is Elbo Room, home of spring break.

The iconic watering hole opened its doors in 1938 and bore witness to the rebellious '50s and groovy '60s, when Fort Lauderdale experienced a boom of northerners who heard about this place in South Florida that served beer and fruity cocktails. The dive bar was even included in the 1960 rom-com *Where the Boys Are*, starring Connie Francis and George Hamilton (which had its movie premiere at the Gateway Theatre, also in Fort Lauderdale).

Today, the bar still attracts throngs of spring breakers, bachelorette parties, visitors, and locals to watch the game or listen to live music while breathing in that salty ocean air. In 1994, Elbo Room claimed to be the first commercial establishment "in the world" to install live cameras, so even when you're back home, you can still tune in on the fun.

After the Florida Panthers won their first Stanley Cup in 2024, the bar was one of the first stops for the team. With the cup in tow, the Cats partied with fans and jumped into the Atlantic Ocean; as frequent visitors to the bar, the players returned to Elbo Room later that week to continue the celebrations.

The Elbo Room was originally called the Seabreeze Restaurant, then its name was changed after World War II.

The Elbo Room bar has been a beach mainstay since its opening in 1938. Courtesy Felix Mizioznikov / Shutterstock.com

ELBO ROOM

WHAT: The bar where spring break was born

WHERE: 241 S Fort Lauderdale Beach Blvd., Fort Lauderdale

COST: Free to enter

PRO TIP: The bar is cash only, so don't forget to make a stop at an ATM.

REST IN PEACE

Where is Leslie Nielsen buried?

Only a comedian would want a fart joke included in his final resting place.

When *The Naked Gun* and *Airplane!* actor and comedian Leslie Nielsen died in Fort Lauderdale in November 2010, he was buried at Evergreen Cemetery, one of the oldest in the city. Even in death, the comedian has people laughing—"Let 'er Rip" is on his brass plaque, a nod to his penchant for fart jokes (he allegedly even had a fart machine to create the sound on demand). Near the plaque is also a memorial bench with a quote from Nielsen: "Sit down whenever you can."

Nielsen has quite the legendary company at Evergreen Cemetery. Frank and Ivy Stranahan—considered the founders of Fort Lauderdale—are buried at the cemetery, alongside other founding families such as the Kings, the Cromarties, and the Moores. It was the Kings who platted a portion of their property to be used as a cemetery, as the riverfront town grew with more families calling it their permanent home. The city purchased 11 acres from 1917 to 1938, and it's considered an honor to be buried in Evergreen

EVERGREEN CEMETERY

WHAT: Where local legends are buried

WHERE: 1300 SE 10th Ave., Fort Lauderdale

COST: Free to enter

PRO TIP: Victims of the Great Miami Hurricane of 1926 were buried in unmarked graves in the north-central section of the cemetery.

Ed and Susan King owned the land the cemetery was built on, eventually selling it to the city in 1917 for $2,000.

Above: *The Stranahans, considered the founders of Fort Lauderdale, are buried at Evergreen Cemetery.*

Left: *The grave of Leslie Nielsen is a popular stop for visitors to the cemetery. Courtesy Ellery Andrews*

Cemetery. A number of veterans, some dating to the Civil War, are at rest here.

Since it was built before the age of the automobile, the cemetery has just one small paved road through the middle, and it can be a bit tough to navigate. But with its towering banyan and oak trees throughout, it's a peaceful, unassuming part of Fort Lauderdale that's worth a visit.

AYE, AYE, CAPTAIN

Where did gamblers, rum runners, and dignitaries hang out?

Hop aboard—you'll need a boat to get to Cap's Place. Open since 1928 (originally known as Club Unique), this supper club once drew local gamblers and rum runners. Today it brings together history buffs and foodies.

The restaurant gets its name from its founder, Captain Theodore "Cap" Knight, considered one of the earlier settlers of Lighthouse Point. He ran away from home at just 13 and worked on boats up and down the east coast of the United States. He married his second wife, Lola Saunders, in 1916, and the couple got involved in rum running—locals would pick up booze in the Bahamas and bring it up to Florida. Cap was known for his fast boats and being able to easily navigate the dark waters between the Bahamas and Florida.

Later, Cap got into the restaurant business and opened Club Unique, with fresh seafood, slot machines, card and dice games, and a Wheel of Fortune. In the early days, guests would flash their lights, signaling to an employee to come retrieve them by rowboat. Dignitaries and celebrities have also dined at

CAP'S PLACE

WHAT: A restaurant you can only access by boat

WHERE: 2765 NE 28th Court, Lighthouse Point

COST: Free to enter

PRO TIP: A local dish the restaurant is famous for is the heart of palm salad, made from the inner core of a palm tree.

Above: *Enjoying dinner at the oldest restaurant in Broward County.*

Opposite: *Explore the walls of the restaurant and bar for hidden details.*

Cap's Place, including President Franklin Delano Roosevelt, Prime Minister Winston Churchill, Joe DiMaggio, George Harrison, and the Vanderbilts.

These days, patrons hop on a boat from across the Intracoastal that travels back and forth through the evening. Make time to explore the old bar and take in all the ephemera on the walls, from old Florida paintings to World War II–era signage and rusting cash registers.

The walls are covered with historic memorabilia, including a Certificate of War Necessity for the restaurant from World War II.

WHAT A WRECK

Where do divers go to see shipwrecks?

Venture into the depths of the Atlantic Ocean off the coast of Pompano Beach—there's a whole other world underwater. At Shipwreck Park visitors can explore a series of sunken vessels and artificial and natural reefs. In fact, the city just north of Fort Lauderdale has been dubbed the Wreck Capital of Florida for all of the experiences available for scuba divers and snorkelers alike.

Some wrecks of note include the *Lady Luck*, a 324-foot-long ship that was sunk in 2016 and includes a comical sculpture of sharks gathered around a poker table and *Pirate's Treasure Chest* by artist Donald Gialanella. These

Exploring the engine room of the Lady Luck *at Shipwreck Park. Photos courtesy Jimmy Gadomski*

Local divers celebrate the holidays together underwater, including diving with Santa, watching Fourth of July fireworks from a boat, and spooky dives for Halloween.

SHIPWRECK PARK

WHAT: A secret world under the sea

WHERE: Pompano Beach coast

COST: Varies by boat company

PRO TIP: Sculptures are often on display on land for photos before being sunk for divers.

Above: *A diver stands guard at Shipwreck Park.*

Left: *A pirate flag flies from the stern of the* Okinawa.

art installations create a unique diving experience, and new ideas are always in the works.

Also at Shipwreck Park is the SS *Copenhagen*, a British cargo steamer that struck a reef in 1900 while delivering black coal. The crew was forced to abandon the ship, and it's now one of 11 Florida underwater archaeological preserves. For many years, the ship was above water, and it was used for target practice during World War II. Today, it's an artificial reef with spiny lobsters, dazzling tropical fish, small lumps of coal, and spent ammunition shells.

While Shipwreck Park has the greatest number of wrecks in the area, they're part of a collection of more than 100 reefs and shipwrecks off the 23 miles of coastline in Greater Fort Lauderdale. For example, the *Guy Harvey* is a popular wreck named for the beloved marine artist who created a mural on the side of the *Lady Kimberly*, a 185-foot-long freighter built in 1957 and sunk in 1997.

MYTHOLOGICAL CREATURES

What's the giant statue outside Gulfstream Park?

You can't miss the massive statue at the entry to Gulfstream Park. The 110-foot-tall statue—a sculpture and fountain of Pegasus trampling a dragon—is the third-tallest statue in the US and territories, behind only the Statue of Liberty in New York City and *Birth of the New World* in Puerto Rico. Made of bronze and steel, it weighs more than 700 tons and was made in pieces in China and Germany.

GULFSTREAM PARK

WHAT: See one of the tallest statues in the US.

WHERE: 901 S Federal Hwy., Hallandale Beach

COST: Free to enter

PRO TIP: The first race at Gulfstream Park was in 1939.

Come for the statue, but stay for the fun. Once inside Gulfstream Park, visitors can take part in betting on horse racing, shopping, and dining. The races take place 10 months out of the year, including major tournaments like the Pegasus World Cup and Florida Derby. During these live race days, sit in the stands or watch from the comfort of a dining table at Ten Palms, which overlooks the track that measures a little more than 1 mile in circumference. Another fun destination within Gulfstream Park is the Carousel Club, an alfresco bar made from a moving carousel at the edge of the track.

New to horse racing? Racing ambassadors at Gulfstream's guest services booth are on hand to guide newbies through the basics of the sport and help with the self-service wagering machines.

Pegasus and Dragon *is the third-tallest statue in the US and territories. Courtesy YES Market Media / Shutterstock.com*

The idea for the statue came from Frank Stronach, who owns Gulfstream Park, then executed by German design company Strassacker.

THE MYSTERY OF FLIGHT 19

What happened to 27 pilots?

With more than 35 million travelers passing through Fort Lauderdale–Hollywood International Airport, it's one of the busiest in the nation. However, there is one storied flight that still has the military scratching its heads.

In December 1945 the airport was the site of the US Naval Air Station Fort Lauderdale, and five TBM Avenger torpedo bombers set off for a routine training flight. The experienced Lt. Charles C. Taylor was the flight leader. He planned to lead Flight 19 through practice bombing runs in the Keys, fly to Grand Bahama Island, and then return to Fort Lauderdale. However, things started to go wrong for the second leg of the flight.

NAVAL AIR STATION FORT LAUDERDALE MUSEUM

WHAT: Remember the fighter pilots who took off and never returned.

WHERE: 4000 W Perimeter Rd., Fort Lauderdale

COST: Free entry, donations appreciated

PRO TIP: The museum has a butterfly garden designed by veterans with a memorial to Flight 19.

Taylor called the Fort Lauderdale flight tower with a series of confusing messages that he "cannot see land." He disappeared for 10 minutes, and according to the Naval History and Heritage Command, a voice that was not Taylor's called and said, "We can't find west. Everything is wrong. We can't be sure of any direction. Everything looks strange, even the ocean." 20 minutes later, an unknown pilot told the tower in a voice that was "trembling, bordering on hysteria." He said, "We can't tell where we are . . . everything is . . .

The pilots of the missing Flight 19 were flying the same kind of aircraft pictured here, the Grumman TBM Avenger. Courtesy Naval History and Heritage Command

can't make out anything. We think we may be about 225 miles northeast of base. . . ." with the final words, "It looks like we are entering white water. . . . We're completely lost."

Two PBM Mariner flying boats went out for a rescue mission, but the tower lost contact with those planes, too. Another round of rescue teams went out and searched for five days and couldn't find a single sign of any of the aircraft over 250,000 square miles of the Atlantic Ocean and the Gulf of Mexico. In all, 27 men from Flight 19 and the PBM Mariner rescue flights were lost, and what happened that day remains a mystery.

President George H. W. Bush trained at US Naval Air Station Fort Lauderdale when he was 19 years old, piloting the Avenger Torpedo Bomber.

A FARM IN FORT LAUDERDALE

What restaurant has the longest reservation wait?

As of this writing, the wait to get a table at Regina's Farm was a whopping four years. That's right, a whole presidential term will have passed by the time a guest can make their way into this urban farm that has clearly had people talking.

An urban farm hidden away in the heart of Fort Lauderdale, Regina Rodrigues welcomes the public to her backyard to dine buffet-style on hearty plates of polenta, chicken, beef, rice, vegetables, soups, desserts, and her famous cheese bread, or pão de queijo. While waiting to eat, little ones hop aboard a train set weaving through the yard. Chickens meander through the crowd and the smells of dinner waft from the brick stove as Rodrigues puts the final touches on the dishes. Once she announces that it's dinner time, everyone sits communally at picnic tables. South Florida might be known for quick outbursts of rain, but Rodrigues and her family will usher guests into their living room to wait out the storm. It doesn't get more

REGINA'S FARM

WHAT: A backyard Brazilian dinner made by your new friend

WHERE: 1101 Middle St., Fort Lauderdale

COST: Flat dinner fee for entry

PRO TIP: If you want to have alcohol with your dinner, it's BYOB at Regina's Farm.

Proceeds from the dinner go toward the neighborhood, Las Olas Worship Center, and other churches and community groups.

Above: *Regina Rodrigues prepares a feast for her guests each weekend. Photos courtesy Caio Martins Rodrigues*

Left: *Regina Rodrigues*

family style than this, and Brazilian transplants have put their stamp of approval on Rodrigues's cooking.

The casual backyard restaurant is open most Saturdays and Sundays, and guests need to text or message the restaurant on Facebook to make a reservation. Don't expect one any time soon, though. Dinner at Regina's Farm books up years in advance, so get on the waiting list in the event someone cancels their reservation.

NEVER FORGET

Where can you find a piece of the World Trade Center?

Decades have passed since September 11, 2001, but the tragedies in New York City, Washington, DC, and Pennsylvania are still with us—and with so many transplants from the Northeast living in Fort Lauderdale, it's a solemn day that is remembered annually.

Fort Lauderdale was one of several places across the country to get pieces of the World Trade Center to create monuments. The first was dedicated at the Fort Lauderdale–Hollywood International Airport on September 11, 2016, inside the lower level of Terminal 1 by baggage claim. Here visitors can see a piece of the South Tower, a helmet from a New York Fire Department firefighter who was a part of the rescue efforts, and a donated American flag from Air Force Lt. Col. (Ret.) Michael F. Janzen. The fragment of the South Tower is small in size, but it is encased in a floor-to-ceiling pillar and flanked by two American flags.

Four years later, the city received a second piece of the World Trade Center, which was dedicated at the Riverwalk on September 11, 2020. The monument, overlooking the New River, is made from a piece of the PATH train tracks built in 1909. The section is supported by three vertical granite pillars

WORLD TRADE CENTER MEMORIALS

WHAT: Remember 9/11 with two monuments.

WHERE: Riverwalk 9/11 Monument, south of the intersection of Southwest First Ave. and West Las Olas Blvd.; 9/11 Memorial at Airport, 100 Terminal Dr., Fort Lauderdale

COST: Free to enter

PRO TIP: Each year on September 11, Fort Lauderdale hosts a moving memorial service at the Riverwalk monument to pay tribute to the 2,977 people killed.

Above: *The monument overlooking the New River was made of a piece of the PATH train tracks. Photos courtesy Middle River Arts Photography*

Left: *The flag flies at half-staff at the memorial commemorating the lives lost on September 11, 2001.*

and joined by an acrylic spine, all representing the strength of Manhattan as well as the light in darkness. It also conveys a sense of volunteerism, as three firefighters drove to New York City to pick up the PATH track and bring it down to Fort Lauderdale.

> With so many transplants from New York living in Fort Lauderdale, the terrorist attacks personally affected many residents locally.

WHAT'S IN A NAME?

Where did Fort Lauderdale get its name?

Just by its name, it's pretty obvious that Fort Lauderdale was named after a fort. But who was the fort named after? A man named Major William M. Lauderdale, who spent all of a month in the area.

Lauderdale was born in Virginia in 1782 and came from a prestigious military family—his father and uncle fought alongside George Washington, and Lauderdale himself was commissioned as a first lieutenant in 1812 by future president Andrew Jackson. He was living in Tennessee at the time and fought in numerous battles in the South; in fact, Jackson called for his help after being defeated by indigenous troops in Alabama. He started a family when he was 40, marrying twice and having five children.

In 1837, his military smarts were needed again, this time in Florida. Major General Thomas Jesup asked Lauderdale to join him to battle in the Seminole Wars, and Jackson wrote a letter in support, saying "I know of but one man I think can raise a battalion." Lauderdale headed to Florida, bringing with him five Tennessee volunteer companies, with a mission to march south to create a safe passageway. They built a fort on the New River, called Fort Lauderdale, and faced off with Seminole soldiers led by Sam Jones in Pine Island Ridge in present day Davie for the final battle of the Seminole Wars.

Lauderdale died soon after, and an honorable discharge celebration in Louisiana was turned into a funeral. The

---

In Fort Lauderdale, there is a small park (less than 1 acre) named Major William M. Lauderdale Park.

A statue of Major William M. Lauderdale stands outside of the Forest Ridge neighborhood in Davie. Courtesy Felix Mizioznikov / Shutterstock.com

City of Fort Lauderdale was incorporated in 1911, keeping the name, and a bronze statue of the major by Luis Montoya was erected in 1988 in Davie.

FORT LAUDERDALE ORIGINS

WHAT: Meet the major after whom Fort Lauderdale is named.

WHERE: West of Pine Island Road in Davie, at the Intersection of Forest Ridge Boulevard and Forest Ridge Circle outside of the Forest Ridge neighborhood

COST: Free to enter

PRO TIP: The original Fort Lauderdale was abandoned, but the name remained with the fort as it relocated two more times, each time moving east.

A ROYAL WELCOME

Are there nobles in Fort Lauderdale?

Major William Lauderdale was a descendant of the Lauderdale family in Scotland, and his cousins happened upon the town by accident.

In 1905, Gwendolyn Maitland, countess of Lauderdale, was boating down the New River during a visit to Florida when she asked a man on the shore for the name of the village they were passing. She thought it was a joke when he said, "Fort Lauderdale." In February of 1925, while spending the winter in Palm Beach (as many of the rich and famous still do), the countess wrote a letter to Mayor Will J. Reed, asking to visit. The town was ecstatic at the thought of European nobility coming to visit, and they laid out the red carpet for her and her husband, the Earl of Lauderdale. "Until 6 o'clock they were entertained by the mayor with drives through the city, visiting Las Olas and other points of interest," according to the *Fort Lauderdale Daily News*. She told the newspaper "I am proud of the city that bears our ancient name."

A VISIT FROM FORT LAUDERDALE NOBILITY

WHAT: The Rainbow Roof Garden

WHERE: The restaurant no longer exists, but it was on Las Olas Blvd., a major shopping and dining thoroughfare in downtown Fort Lauderdale.

COST: Free to enter

PRO TIP: Club Floranada never came to be, although Floranada Elementary School and Floranada Park are in Fort Lauderdale.

The couple became investors in the Floranada Club, a resort in the works just outside of the town. In 1926 the countess and earl returned to Fort Lauderdale for a more formal visit with a banquet planned at the Rainbow Roof Garden. "It is to be a civic event to which every person in Fort Lauderdale is invited, and at the request of the Countess the nature of the ceremony will be entirely informal," the *Fort*

COUNTESS TELLS OF LOVE FOR LAUDERDALE

RIO-VISTA

Top: *The Countess of Lauderdale is given a royal welcome by Fort Lauderdale residents. Photos courtesy History Fort Lauderdale*

Left: *The Countess of Lauderdale's visit to Fort Lauderdale makes the front page of the* Fort Lauderdale Daily News.

Right: *The Countess of Lauderdale receives a key to the city during her visit to Fort Lauderdale.*

Lauderdale Daily News reported. On the schedule: invocation, quartet choir, reading of a historical sketch, the audience singing "God Save the King," and presenting the countess with a key to the city. The local radio station aired the event using "the most powerful amplifier" with hopes it could be broadcast across the country and across the pond.

Gwendolyn Maitland once again made the front page of the paper when she died in Palm Beach in 1929.

TARPON AND TORPEDOES

Can you eat at a secret submarine base?

15th Street Fisheries and the Lauderdale Marina are Fort Lauderdale institutions, run by the Cox family since the 1940s. Once upon a time, though, the site was a secret military research station.

From 1942 to 1946, pilots trained to fly torpedo bombers—among them President George H. W. Bush, who graduated from the Naval Air Station Fort Lauderdale in 1943. Working with torpedoes was dangerous work, and 94 trainees were killed during exercises. By 1946 the war was over, but the area was still leased to the US military. Engineer (and future Fort Lauderdale mayor) Robert O. Cox saw that it was prime real estate for a marina, and after negotiating with the landowner he opened the Lauderdale Marina in 1948; in 1978 the Cox family opened 15th Street Fisheries.

In fact, there was a battle over a torpedo between Cox and the US Navy. In 1956 Cox hired 16-year-old twin boys John and Charles Noyes to search for a torpedo to put on display, knowing the history of the area. He told the *Miami Herald*, "It's my torpedo and I'm going to fight for it all the way to Washington." Cox ended up deciding he didn't want it after all, that it was too rusted.

The family-owned restaurant is known for its pool of tarpon that come in for feedings. Kids and kids at heart can feed the giant fish at the dock—they can grow to be 8 feet

---

15th Street Fisheries is accessible by boat, including the Water Taxi; it's stop No. 3 on its route.

A view of 15th Street Fisheries and the surrounding area, once a secret military site. Courtesy Felix Mizioznikov / Shutterstock.com

long and weigh 300 pounds. As for the dining experience (tarpon is not on the menu—the bony flesh has made it an unpopular seafood dish), there is a casual dockside diner that offers live music, and the more formal upstairs dining room is designed to look like a boat house. Dishes include conch chowder, fried gator, grilled swordfish, pan-seared cobia, and other oh-so-Florida fare.

15TH STREET FISHERIES

WHAT: A top-secret torpedo station turned marina and restaurant

WHERE: 1900 SE 15th St., Fort Lauderdale

COST: Free to enter

PRO TIP: The bait shop on site has packs of frozen shrimp for purchase to toss to the tarpon, if you want more than what the staff has on hand.

VIKTOR E. FOR THE FLORIDA PANTHERS

Why do they throw rubber rats onto the rink?

Cheers, fist pumps, and a rubber rodent thrown onto the rink—it's how you celebrate a win for the Florida Panthers hockey team.

Athletes are known for having superstitions, and this one started back in 1996 when the Cats were set to play the Calgary Flames in the opener for their third season. Forward Scott Mellanby killed a rat in the locker room with his hockey stick before they took the ice at the Miami Arena (now the Kaseya Center, home of the Miami Heat basketball team). The team ended up winning 4–3, with Mellanby scoring two of the Panthers' goals. Goaltender John Vanbiesbrouck dubbed it "a rat trick," and it became tradition for the crowd to throw plastic rats onto the rink whenever the Panthers scored a goal.

As you can imagine, that led to lag time in the game as staff had to clean up the rink multiple times per game. The National Hockey League wound up banning the practice. Hockey fans are known for being of the rebellious sort, though, and the tradition continues, but now the rats are thrown onto the rink at the end of a winning game.

FLORIDA PANTHERS

WHAT: Celebrate a victory with a rubber rat.

WHERE: Amerant Bank Arena, 1 Panther Pkwy., Sunrise

COST: Ticket prices vary

PRO TIP: The arena is across the street from Sawgrass Mills Mall, the largest outlet mall in the country. Locals will often grab dinner at one of the mall's many sit-down restaurants and then walk to the arena for a Panthers game or concert.

The Florida Panthers take to the ice at the Amerant Bank Arena in Sunrise. Courtesy YES Market Media / Shutterstock.com

Rats are so much a part of the Panthers' psyche, though, that a second mascot was added to the roster in 2014: Viktor E. Ratt.

The tradition got national attention when the Florida Panthers won their first Stanley Cup in 2024, leading to news articles explaining the odd habit. The team took the cup on a raucous tour of the city after its win, including a dip into the Atlantic Ocean at Fort Lauderdale Beach, filling it with beer at Elbo Room, and eating a hearty helping of pasta out of it at Heritage restaurant.

Viktor E. Ratt is known to bust a move on the ice, as well as dancing with fans in the stands.

SWEET NOSTALGIA

Where can you get candy cigarettes?

Did you know the candy cigarettes that blow smoke are made in Macedonia? And that the sticks are manufactured in Colombia? Antonio Dumas, a self-proclaimed candyologist, knows this and much more.

He's the owner of To the Moon, a unique marketplace of nostalgia in Wilton Manors, where he's been strutting his candy smarts since 2005. More than 13,000 items are for sale at To the Moon, from candies and potato chips to lava lamps, greeting cards, and even action figures of the late Pope Francis and US Supreme Court Justice Ruth Bader Ginsburg. In the fridge you can find pints of Jeni's Ice Creams, an Ohio brand that churns out flavors like Sweet Cream Biscuits & Peach Jam, Goat Cheese with Red Berries, Brown Butter Almond Brittle, and other sweet delights. Then there are the hard-to-find sodas, like Sun Drop, Cheerwine, and RC Cola.

TO THE MOON

WHAT: A one-stop shop for imported and old-school candy

WHERE: 2205 Wilton Dr., Wilton Manors

COST: Free to enter

PRO TIP: Wilton Drive is worth a walk for its shops, restaurants, bars, and public art.

But what To the Moon is best known for is its selection of candies, including retro throwbacks from brands dating back to 1806. Think Clark bars, Mallo Cups, candy buttons, Oh Henry, Turkish Taffy, Sanders fudge, Pop Rocks, candy cigarettes, and endless varieties of chocolates and licorice. Items are imported from 90 countries, so you'll be getting authentic German Haribo gummy candies and cookies from Italy. As customers stroll the aisles, music from the '50s and '60s plays overhead, setting the scene for a walk (and taste) down memory lane.

Top Left: *A rack of gummy candy at To the Moon.*

Top Right: *It's hard to miss the brightly colored entrance to To the Moon on Wilton Drive.*

Left: *To the Moon is filled with candies and gifts.*

To the Moon has everything you need for a unique gift, including a massive selection of greeting cards that will make you chuckle.

BE KIND, REWIND

Where did the owner of Blockbuster live?

The first Blockbuster store may have opened in Dallas, but the company's headquarters and owner were right here in Fort Lauderdale.

H. Wayne Huizenga purchased the iconic video company in 1986, a year after its founding. Under his management, Blockbuster became the Friday night plan for millions. In 1992, the world headquarters opened in Fort Lauderdale (at Las Olas Boulevard and Andrews Avenue) in a celebration that included Huizenga carrying around the green street sign among revelers. Longtime Greater Fort Lauderdale residents will also remember Blockbuster Golf & Games in Sunrise, an arcade and entertainment center from 1996 to 2000.

Today, at History Fort Lauderdale, visitors can see a tribute to Blockbuster and Huizenga in a display case. There's a blue-and-yellow case commemorating $150 million in Blockbuster stock as well as a signed Miami Dolphins football from the team's 1972 perfect season. After all, Huizenga owned the team—as well as the Florida Marlins (now the Miami Marlins) and the Florida Panthers, as well as AutoNation and Waste Management.

The Huizengas' legacy has lived on in Fort Lauderdale, with his name and that of his wife, Marti, sprinkled throughout the city. There's Huizenga Park in downtown, the Marti Huizenga Club Boys & Girls Clubs of Broward County, and the Huizenga Pavilion at the Broward Center (where you can also dine at Marti's New River Bistro), just to name a few.

Blockbuster relocated its headquarters in 1996, from Fort Lauderdale to Dallas, Texas.

A commemorative Blockbuster video to mark $150 million in Blockbuster stock. Courtesy History Fort Lauderdale

Sadly, the last Blockbuster video in the country closed in 2019, but its memory lives on at History Fort Lauderdale.

HISTORY FORT LAUDERDALE

WHAT: A tribute to the blue-and-yellow video tape

WHERE: 231 SW 2nd Ave., Fort Lauderdale

COST: There is a small fee for entry, and tours can be booked at an additional cost.

PRO TIP: Check out the artists' lofts in the museum.

BEAM ME UP, SCOTTY

What is that spaceship building on Federal Highway?

It's a landmark in Fort Lauderdale, having landed on Federal Highway back in the 1960s, but by the looks of it, it arrived from a galaxy far, far away.

Known as the KenAnn building, it was built in 1964 and designed by local architect Louis F. Wolff. Its circular shape, spiky crown, blue tile, concave mural, and sea of windows all give it the look of a futuristic abode—and local lore that it was inspired by *The Jetsons*. The owners were Ken and Ann Burnstine (hence the name) and they opened the nightclub Chateau Madrid on the top floor.

Ken was a Marine pilot turned drug smuggler, and the AP called him "one of America's most daring drug smugglers" in a 1981 article. However, in 1976, he died in a plane crash in the Mojave Desert while working with federal prosecutors after being sentenced to seven years in prison for his role in a $50 million trafficking ring in Fort Lauderdale.

While the Burnstines are no longer with us, their KenAnn building is still a landmark at the border of Oakland Park

KENANN BUILDING

WHAT: A space-age design landmark

WHERE: 3101 N Federal Hwy., Oakland Park

COST: Free to enter

PRO TIP: Inside, the space theme continues with the floor tiles and galaxy-blue walls.

Other nightclubs that would call the KenAnn Building home over the years included The Rooftop and Hot Chocolate.

Above: *The KenAnn Building on US 1 was named for its original owners, Ken and Ann Burnstine.*

Left: *The tilework on the KenAnn Building showcases bits of Florida from orange groves to marine animals.*

and Fort Lauderdale that you can't miss. Today, it's home to a Citibank branch office and a gym, among other tenants, and as development continues in the area, it's joining the campus of Oaklyn, a mixed-use block with apartments and businesses.

BRUSH WITH FATE

Where can you find paintings from the Florida Highwaymen?

Countless people walk through the lobby of Oakland Park City Hall, passing six landscape paintings hanging from the walls. What they may not realize is that these pieces are worth tens of thousands of dollars thanks to the unassuming painters who have made Florida history.

They're the works of the Florida Highwaymen, a group of 26 black painters who in the 1960s and '70s made their living by selling their paintings on South Florida roadways from the trunks of their cars. They were known for their landscapes, capturing the wild and wonderful side of Florida's lush swamps, palm trees, beaches, and fiery sunsets.

In the early '70s, Oakland Park's longtime city clerk, Darlene Mitchell, helped to purchase a few dozen paintings from the Florida Highwaymen. However, when city hall was under renovation in 1990, the paintings were stored away and forgotten about. They were rediscovered in 2003 and have been on display ever since.

More paintings by the Florida Highwaymen are hung in city hall chambers.

Two paintings by the Florida Highwaymen in the lobby of Oakland Park City Hall

OAKLAND PARK CITY HALL

WHAT: Rare Florida Highwaymen paintings on display

WHERE: 3650 NE 12th Ave., Oakland Park

COST: Free to enter

PRO TIP: Ask to check out the painting inside the commission chambers, too.

Oakland Park City Hall has six paintings, and the Ethel M. Gordon Oakland Park Library has four. Of special note is that the city has a painting by MaryAnne Carroll, the lone woman painter among the Florida Highwaymen. She told the *Sun Sentinel* in 2003 that it was a "survival" hobby to earn money to feed her seven children. She nailed canvases to a backyard in her tree and used it as her easel.

In 2004, the state inducted the 26 artists into the Florida Artists Hall of Fame, grouping them as the Original Florida Highwaymen—including one Highwaywoman, of course.

Works by the Florida Highwaymen can also be found at the Museum of Florida History in Tallahassee and the National Museum of American History and Culture in Washington, DC.

A FEAT OF ENGINEERING

Where was the first tunnel in Florida built?

There aren't too many underwater tunnels in all of Florida, let alone South Florida. In fact, there are just two—including the Kinney Tunnel in Fort Lauderdale, which was the first.

Before the tunnel, locals relied on the Federal Aid Highway Bridge, a drawbridge that connected one side of the river to the other beginning in 1926. However, as Fort Lauderdale started to grow, city planners proposed building a tunnel under the New River. The idea seemed wild, considering that Fort Lauderdale has a high water table. Ivy Stranahan, one of the founders of Fort Lauderdale, was particularly opposed to the idea since her iconic green-and-white house would sit on top of the tunnel.

However, the project was approved, and when it opened in 1960 as the New River Tunnel it was the first tunnel in the state of Florida, built at a whopping cost of $15 million—about $160 million today. New technology was implemented for the project, and it was even proposed as "the biggest hurricane

KINNEY TUNNEL

WHAT: The first tunnel in Florida

WHERE: Federal Highway just south of Las Olas Boulevard in downtown Fort Lauderdale

COST: Free to enter

PRO TIP: There are only two public underwater tunnels in Florida; the other is at the Port of Miami.

On top of the tunnel is the fittingly named Tunnel Top Plaza, a green space with seating, trees, and great views of downtown and the New River.

The Henry. E. Kinney Tunnel was named for a newspaper editor who was in favor of building the tunnel.

shelter in town." A 1960 *Fort Lauderdale Daily News* article reported, "A resident engineer with 25 years of tunnel building experience says that this was one of the most difficult jobs he ever tackled." In 1986, the tunnel was rededicated as the Henry E. Kinney Tunnel in honor of the editor of the *Miami Herald*'s Fort Lauderdale/Broward bureau; he had written many columns advocating for the tunnel while it was being built. Today, the tunnel is an integral part of navigating downtown.

HOUSE BOAT

Why did a historic house float down the river?

In the historic district of downtown Fort Lauderdale sits a cozy Georgian home fit with a front porch and green shutters. It's the King-Cromartie House, a symbol of the early days of Fort Lauderale.

However, the spot where it sits today is not where it was originally built.

The four-bedroom house was built in 1907 on the south side of the New River by Ed King, made of Dade County pine and salvaged ship timber. His daughter, Louise, married Bloxham Cromartie and the home stayed in the family until 1968.

The age-old fight between development and historic preservation reared its head, threatening to take down the King-Cromartie House. In October 1971, the home was under threat of demolition to make way for condos, so the Junior League of Fort Lauderdale pitched in to pay for the house to be floated down the New River and restored. It was moved by barge and relocated to its current spot in the historic district of the city, on the north side of the river.

The house is now neighbors with a number of other historic spaces, including the 1905 New River Inn (which houses History Fort Lauderdale) and the 1899 Schoolhouse Museum. History Fort Lauderdale offers a three-museum tour of the historic campus, including the King-Cromartie House, where

---

The King-Cromartie House isn't the only historic home that has been relocated locally; neither the Sample-McDougald House nor the McNab House in Pompano Beach are in their original locations.

KING-CROMARTIE HOUSE

WHAT: A historic home that was floated down the river

WHERE: 231 SW Second Ave., Fort Lauderdale

COST: There is an admission fee to enter. Discounts are available for students and seniors.

PRO TIP: Bloxham Cromartie was the brother of Ivy Stranahan, considered the mother of Fort Lauderdale.

Top: *The bridge had to be lifted for the King-Cromartie House to make it to its final destination.*

Below: *The King-Cromartie House in its current location on the north side of the New River. Photos courtesy History Fort Lauderdale*

guests can travel back in time to the early 1900s with clothing, toys, and furnishings on display.

And we can thank the Junior League—which is still very active in the community—for that.

SPIN ME RIGHT ROUND

What is the significance of 66 in Pier Sixty-Six?

With its crown of spires, Pier Sixty-Six could be considered our very own Statue of Liberty—it certainly has drawn the masses over the years.

The hotel, which underwent a major overhaul, got its start as a humble Phillips 66 gas station, an important fueling stop for boaters making their way to the Bahamas. As Fort Lauderdale itself became the destination, Pier Sixty-Six joined the legion of hotels welcoming vacationers from around the world. At the time of its construction, the hotel and marina was the tallest building in Broward County.

When it was built, the designers had fun with the number 66 for Pier Top, the bar and lounge in the iconic tower. It rotated every 66 minutes and took 66 seconds by elevator to reach from the ground floor. The number play does not include the year, though—the 17-story tower opened

PIER SIXTY-SIX PIER TOP LOUNGE

WHAT: 66 reasons to visit Pier Sixty-Six

WHERE: 2301 SE 17th St., Fort Lauderdale

COST: Free to enter

PRO TIP: Pier Sixty-Six consists of both hotel suites as well as residential units.

Fishermen show off their catch in the early days of the marina. Courtesy Pier Sixty-Six

Above: *The new Pier Sixty-Six, which kept nods to the original design. Courtesy Barry Grossman Photography*

Right: *An aerial view of the Pier Sixty-Six back when it opened in 1965. Courtesy Pier Sixty-Six*

its doors in 1965 (apparently waiting another year was not an option). Over the decades, it became a classic Fort Lauderdale destination, hosting many honeymooners, parties, and celebrities such as Frank Sinatra and Walter Cronkite.

Unfortunately, Hurricane Irma rolled through South Florida in 2017 and caused major damage to Pier Sixty-Six, leading to a temporary shutdown for renovations under new ownership. It reopened to much excitement in 2025, especially Pier Top. The rotating bar and lounge is embedded in the DNA of Fort Lauderdale, and even with the reimagining of the property, the owners kept the design elements that made Pier Sixty-Six, well, the Pier Sixty-Six—the 66 spires and the lounge that revolves once every 66 minutes.

The Phillips 66 gas station is long gone, though, as it was demolished in 1981.

What did it take to get the Pier Sixty-Six to the modern state of luxury that it is today? A $1 billion makeover.

SNOW DAY

Has it ever snowed in Fort Lauderdale?

In a holiday tradition that dates back to 1962, Las Olas Boulevard in downtown Fort Lauderdale is transformed into a winter wonderland with an ice skating rink, children's choirs, local vendors, and Santa's Village. One of the biggest draws, though, is Snow Mountain—a pile of "snow" that kids (and kids at heart) can sled down to get a taste of what it's like up north.

CHRISTMAS ON LAS OLAS

WHAT: A sure way to see "snow" in Fort Lauderdale

WHERE: Las Olas Boulevard in Fort Lauderdale

COST: Free to enter

PRO TIP: While it hasn't snowed in decades, one of the telltale signs of dropping temperatures in Fort Lauderdale is iguanas dropping out of the trees due to being cold stunned (don't worry, they come out of hibernation when the temperatures rise).

It's a novelty because the last time we saw snow was on January 19, 1977. Temperatures dropped below freezing and locals woke up to the slightest dusting of snow. The *Fort Lauderdale Daily News* reported that the newspaper switchboards were clogged with hundreds of callers reporting that they saw snow, and the evening edition front page above the fold was dedicated to the historic moment. "SNOW!" it read in a massive banner headline, with an announcement that Broward County public schools would be canceled the next day to preserve power. "White stuff didn't stick but it was fun for awhile," a staff writer wrote.

And it was all over by 9:30 a.m.

It wasn't all fun, though. Gov. Reuben Askew declared a state of emergency because the low temperatures were wreaking havoc on the citrus and vegetable fields in Florida. In fact, 80,000 migrant workers lost their jobs in the tri-county area because of the cold snap.

Kids sled down Snow Mountain during Christmas on Las Olas, the closest we've gotten to the snow day of 1977. Courtesy Las Olas Association

For most of the country, a dusting of snow is not going to make the 5 o'clock news. But this is Fort Lauderdale, and each year on January 19, news outlets remember that one time it snowed. In the meantime, we'll wait for Christmas on Las Olas for a glimpse of snow.

Even though the Miami International Airport, a reporting site for the National Weather Service, did not see the snow, because of widespread eyewitness reports, the snow was recorded.

MONKEYING AROUND

How did vervets get to Dania Beach?

Florida is known for its odd array of wildlife, from alligators in the Everglades to tiny Key deer in the Florida Keys and green parakeets singing in the palm trees. But in Greater Fort Lauderdale there's a family of vervet monkeys that have made their home in the Port Everglades mangroves and West Park area for almost 100 years.

The vervets were brought to the area in the 1940s for use in the Anthropoid Ape Research Foundation, later bought out and renamed the Dania Chimpanzee Farm. The monkeys were imported from Africa and used for research and entertainment. Apparently the vervets weren't fans of the arrangement, and about a dozen of them managed to escape from the facility and were never retrieved.

DANIA BEACH VERVETS

WHAT: A colony of escaped vervets living their best life

WHERE: The area of West Lake Park and Port Everglades, including LauderAle, 3305 SE 14th Ave., Fort Lauderdale

COST: Free to enter

PRO TIP: The vervets are often spotted hanging out with customers at LauderAle brewery.

Top Left and Opposite: *A member of the vervet colony that calls the Greater Fort Lauderdale area home. Photos courtesy Missy Williams, Dania Beach Monkey Sanctuary*

Top Right: *A vervet mother and baby*

Their offspring have since called the area by the airport and Port Everglades home.

Since the vervets are not native to the area, they're not a protected species—this also goes for other invasive species like iguanas and pythons. Local animal activists created the Dania Beach Vervet Project to create a sanctuary for the monkeys to avoid getting hit by cars, getting electrocuted, or being picked up by unsavory types wanting to put the critters on the pet market. This would also give them a place to recover should they be injured, as they cannot be released into the wild.

A team from Florida Atlantic University published a paper on the vervets in 2021, the first scientific study of the animals and their origins.

HUNTING GROUNDS

Why are there pythons in the Everglades?

Most people are aware of the alligators that call the Everglades and other wetlands home, but pythons also slither beneath the water's surface.

It's a fairly recent phenomenon, with pythons being released into the wild by pet owners or escaping their enclosures. While it may seem innocent, these reptiles can grow up to 18 feet long (the record in Florida!) and have decimated the raccoon, opossum, bobcat and rabbit populations in Everglades National Park. It's a regular news day around here when a python is found attempting to eat an alligator, or even an alligator killing a python. Because these snakes blend in so well in the swamp, it's unclear how many there are out there.

Because of the damage that pythons do to the environment, the state of Florida hosts a 10-day annual Florida Python Challenge, inviting hunters who have completed an online course to take to seven wildlife areas to catch and humanely destroy as many pythons as they can. The prizes are pretty impressive, too—first place for the most pythons removed is $10,000, and there are also military,

BURMESE PYTHONS

WHAT: An unwelcome species in the Florida swamps

WHERE: Big Cypress Wildlife Management Area and the Everglades and Francis S. Taylor Wildlife Management Area, to name a few

COST: Park fees may apply

PRO TIP: Other invasive species in Florida include iguanas, African snails, cane toads, and more.

Scientists estimate there are anywhere from 100,000 to 300,000 Burmese pythons living in the Everglades.

Burmese pythons are invasive to Florida, and once a year the state hosts the Florida Python Challenge, encouraging hunters to capture and kill the snakes. Courtesy Heiko Kiera / Shutterstock.com

professional, and novice prizes with categories such as longest and most pythons.

Not into hunting? There's also a year-round python patrol of counters who can report and photograph sightings of pythons they encounter.

BEWARE OF WHIRLPOOLS

Were there whirlpools in the New River?

The New River in Fort Lauderdale cuts through the city, providing many alfresco diners with waterfront views as well as a waterway for paddleboarders, kayaks, canoes, and yachts making their way through the Venice of America. Once upon a time it also served as a means of transport for trade between European settlers and the Seminole Indian tribe.

There's also plenty of lore around the New River, including the presence of fantastical whirlpools. According to author Donn R. Colee Jr., there were large whirlpools at Sailboat Bend and Tarpon Bend. In 1870, a pioneer surveyor wrote that it was nearly impossible to bypass the whirlpools in boats that used oars.

In a 1943 ad in the *Fort Lauderdale Daily News*, the location of a plot of land was "near the whirlpool on New River, north side." In a 1965 column, "The Beachcomber" Wesley South, wrote of a man named Cropeared Charley, who in 1913 was caught in a whirlpool for hours in a canoe until he was rescued by a Marshal on a motorboat. Most notably, in 1912, the *Lola*, captained by Scott Holloway, was sucked into a whirlpool; he was saved in the nick of time by a dredge boat. He put up a $100 reward for anyone who could find the *Lola*, but it was never recovered.

Fortunately—or unfortunately?—development and the silt that flows into the river has rid the New River of these whirlpools, but they live on in local legend.

Locals gather at the New River, sans whirlpools, for the annual Winterfest boat parade each December.

The New River is a fairly calm waterway, but a century ago, there were legends of whirlpools sucking in boats.

NEW RIVER

WHAT: Legendary whirlpools that took down a boat

WHERE: New River in downtown Fort Lauderdale

COST: Free to enter

PRO TIP: Explore Fort Lauderdale's waterways aboard the Water Taxi, which travels back and forth from Pompano Beach to Hollywood.

SPLENDID SEA COWS

Where is the best place to see manatees?

When you see a lovable manatee up close, it's hard to believe that sailors from centuries ago mistook them for mermaids. They're a regal creature all on their own, but better suited to the "sea cow" nickname.

November 15 marks the arrival of manatee season in Florida, when waters cool down and they seek our warmer temperatures. When the mercury drops—yes, it does get cold from time to time—aggregations of manatees (yes, that's what they're called!) make their way to the warm springs further north in Florida or to the waters surrounding power plants. That includes the Port Everglades power plant in Broward County; it's believed that about 20 percent of Florida manatees spend their time in Broward County. Unfortunately, there's no public viewing space at the power plant (you can drive up to Manatee Lagoon in West Palm Beach for that) but manatees have frequently been seen at the Dania Cutoff Canal, and Sunrise Paddles hosts manatee tours on the Middle River.

SUNRISE PADDLEBOARDS MANATEE TOURS

WHAT: A warm-water refuge for manatees

WHERE: Sunrise Paddleboards, 2520 N Federal Hwy., Fort Lauderdale

COST: Rental fees vary

PRO TIP: Did you find a manatee? Upload a photo to the I Spy a Manatee app.

Manatees are gentle creatures that nosh on seagrass and other plant life they come across; they actually spend about eight hours a day eating. They use their flippers and tails to propel themselves through water, and it's a special treat to see them come up for air (extra points if you find a mama manatee swimming with her babies). It's important to note

Manatee season runs from Nov 15 to March 31. Courtesy William Cushman / Shutterstock.com

that as a protected species, manatees are never to be touched, fed, or watered, and boaters need to take special care to slow down.

Manatee season comes to a close on March 31, when they return as far west as Texas and as far north as Massachusetts.

Broward County is one of 13 counties in Florida with a Manatee Protection Plan, protecting manatees from boats and other vessels.

BLOW ME AWAY

Where can you learn to blow glass from a reality TV contestant?

With a mix of fire, spinning rods, and the hiss of water on molten glass, there's magic being made in Hollywood's ArtsPark. It's Brenna Baker's Hollywood Hot Glass, a studio for experts as well as students that she opened in 2013.

Her journey with glass started at just 14 years old when she took classes at the lauded Corning Museum of Glass in New York, and she's since spent a year with Italian glassmakers in Murano, launched glassblowing programming aboard the Celebrity Equinox and Eclipse cruise ships, and competed on a season of Netflix's *Blown Away*.

For those eager to try something new and out of the ordinary, Hollywood Hot Glass hosts group and private classes where you can create a bowl, a sea turtle, a heart, flowers, soap dispensers, and other pieces of art. Instructors will guide you through choosing the color, working it in the furnace, blowing it to the right shape, working at the bench, and cooling it. Students can pick up their pieces at another date when they're ready to go home. Beware, because you'll be back for more.

HOLLYWOOD HOT GLASS

WHAT: Learn the art of glass blowing from a pro.

WHERE: Hollywood Hot Glass at Young Circle, One Young Cir., Hollywood

COST: Prices for classes vary, but typically start at $60

PRO TIP: Wear closed-toe shoes for your glass class.

Hollywood Hot Glass also hosts classes aboard Celebrity Cruises, where cruisers can make one of eight glass creations.

Above: *Brenna Baker runs Hollywood Hot Glass, offering glass-blowing classes to create all sorts of objects. Courtesy Hollywood Hot Glass*

Right: *The author tries her hand at blowing glass with Brenna Baker.*

Hollywood Hot Glass is located within ArtsPark at Young Circle, a space buzzing with creativity thanks to the art and dance studios, gallery spaces, and amphitheater. Visitors can also enjoy the dog park, green space, playground, splash pad, and other outdoor fun.

TELLING TIME

What's the sculpture in front of the science museum?

Need the time? Just check out the 52-foot-tall display in front of the Museum of Discovery and Science in downtown Fort Lauderdale.

It's the Great Gravity Clock, and standing beneath the kinetic sculpture visitors can tell time with the clanking of balls running through a series of three rails. The bottom tells the hour, the middle has 10-minute balls, and on the top are minute balls. As time passes, balls are released into each rail and are added up to tell time. For example, if there is one ball on each rail, it would be 1:11. The clock was installed at the museum in 1993 and is one of just three gravity clocks in the world—the other two are in Mexico and Japan.

And all that's before you've even walked through the front doors. Inside, visitors are greeted by the gaping mouth of a life-size Megalodon. It's one of the largest on display, making it the perfect photo op (a grown adult can

GREAT GRAVITY CLOCK

WHAT: Get up close with one of just three gravity clocks in the world.

WHERE: Museum of Discovery and Science, 401 SW Second St., Fort Lauderdale

COST: There is an admission fee to enter. Discounts are available for students and seniors.

PRO TIP: There is no entry fee to see the gravity clock, but the museum is worth a visit once you're there!

A popular experience at the museum is the two-story otter habitat, where the playful North American river otters play in their swimming pool and waterfall.

The gravity clock uses a series of balls and rails to tell time. Courtesy Museum of Discovery and Science

easily fit inside the mouth). One of the newer experiences at the museum is the world's first MAGNA-TILES studio, with more than 10,000 magnetic tiles that kids and kids at heart can use to build into anything their imagination can conjure. Finally, the museum's IMAX theatre is home to Florida's largest movie screen, at a staggering six stories tall. Catch a movie or travel through space in one of the museum's science films, outfitted with laser projections and 2D and 3D images.

If you're not sure how much time you have until the next movie, step outside and check the Great Gravity Clock.

TINY TOWN

Where can you see a miniature town?

Get a taste of what it felt like to be Gulliver when he washed ashore on the island of Lilliput. At Safety Town, adults are likely to be taller than any of the buildings here.

SAFETY TOWN

WHAT: A miniature town that'll have you feeling like a giant

WHERE: Welleby Park, 11100 NW 44th St., Sunrise

COST: Free to enter

PRO TIP: Welleby Park is 29 acres and includes playgrounds, a running/walking path, a dog park, a splash pad, a Little Free Library, and a lake.

The tiny town is located in the city of Sunrise's Welleby Park, a public park west of Fort Lauderdale with splash pads, playgrounds, a Little Free Library, walking paths, and other family fun. One of the newer additions to the park is Safety Town, a miniature neighborhood based on facilities throughout Sunrise. Drop off mail at the post office, stop by the dentist's office for a cleaning, pick up groceries from the market, or report a crime at the police station (well, hopefully not). Don't forget to return books to the library, take out money at the bank's ATM, or make an appointment with the veterinarian.

Little ones can walk on the sidewalk or ride their scooters, bicycles, or electric cars down the roads. It's also a good opportunity to learn the rules of the road—there are working traffic lights as well as a railroad crossing at the train tracks. And yes, there's a play train set on the tracks that children can climb on with interactive elements.

Many of the City of Sunrise's annual events are hosted at Welleby Park, including the Fall Harvest Festival.

Safety Town in Welleby Park includes miniature buildings, sidewalks, and even traffic lights. Courtesy Jared Blaut / City of Sunrise

LADY OF THE HOUSE

What cocktail would you serve for visiting guests?

Overlooking the Atlantic Ocean in Fort Lauderdale is the stately Bonnet House, one of the most beloved homes in the area, which has drawn visitors and many school field trips for decades. Before it was a historic home, though, it served as an escape for an artistic couple who enjoyed entertaining guests with their signature cocktail.

The home is named for the bonnet lily that grows in the slough, and the land was a wedding gift in 1920 to artist Frederic Clay Bartlett and his wife, Helen Birch, from her father Hugh Taylor Birch (a state park nearby is named after him). Unfortunately, Helen died of breast cancer in 1925, never seeing their winter home completed. Grieving, Bartlett didn't spend much time at the home until 1931, when he married his second wife, Evelyn Fortune Lilly. Together, the couple transformed the home with their artwork, as well as paintings they collected from renowned artists like Georges Seurat, Paul Gauguin, and Pablo Picasso.

Evelyn Fortune Lilly Bartlett

When they entertained guests, Evelyn was fond of serving them her own creation, the Rangpur Lime Cocktail. Rangpur lime trees still grow in the Bonnet House's citrus orchard; Frederic and Helen brought the rangpur tree back home to Fort Lauderdale with them after a trip to India. The

Evelyn Fortune Lilly Bartlett's creation, a Rangpur Lime Cocktail. Photos courtesy Bonnet House

BONNET HOUSE

WHAT: An artists' abode with a history of a welcome cocktail

WHERE: 900 N Birch Rd., Fort Lauderdale

COST: There is an admission fee to enter. Prices vary, but children 5 and younger go free.

PRO TIP: Evelyn's at The Four Seasons Fort Lauderdale is named for the lady of the Bonnet House, and its Rangpur Daiquiri is a nod to her concoction. The Third Wife is also named in her honor; Frederic Clay Bartlett was twice a widower before their marriage.

fruit can be easily mistaken for an orange. When fully ripe, the pulp is orange, but tastes bitter, like a lime, so Evelyn added maple syrup to sweeten the drink.

The recipe: 4 parts Barbados Eclipse dark rum (150 proof), 1 part fresh rangpur lime juice, and maple syrup to taste. Combine the rum and lime juice in a pitcher, mix well, add enough syrup to sweeten, and chill until ready to serve on ice in a short glass.

Sign up for a class at the Bonnet House, such as yoga on the veranda or orchid care in the greenhouse.

IT'S A BIRD, IT'S A PLANE, IT'S A BLIMP

Where can you see the Goodyear blimp?

From the Rose Bowl to Pebble Beach and SXSW, the Goodyear blimp is nearly as much a part of the entertainment as the football players or musicians. Goodyear commemorated its centenary in 2025 with a blimp celebration in 100 cities around the country.

One place where the blimp is a common site is Greater Fort Lauderdale, particularly Pompano Beach. The beach city is home to one of just four bases for the company, and Wingfoot Two takes residence at the Pompano Beach Airport. The base opened in Pompano Beach in 1979, making it a welcome part of the sky. Some stats on this flying machine: It's 246.6 feet long, 57.71 feet high, and travels at a maximum speed of 73 mph.

In 2016, Wingfoot Two became the first Goodyear Blimp in more than 50 years to be used as a jump platform for skydivers—the US Air Force Academy Wings of Blue team parachuted over the Bristol Motor Speedway.

GOODYEAR BLIMP AIRPARK

WHAT: One of three Goodyear bases in the nation

WHERE: 1500 NE Fifth Ave., Pompano Beach

COST: Free to enter

PRO TIP: For prime views, play a round of golf at the Pompano Beach Golf Course, which is adjacent to the airpark.

The other American blimp bases are near Akron, Ohio, and Los Angeles, California, named Wingfoot One and Three, respectively.

The Goodyear Blimp is a common sight in the sky throughout Greater Fort Lauderdale. Courtesy Goodyear

While the airpark is not open to the public, you'll often see the Goodyear blimp flying overhead as it makes its way to special events around the nation. Locally, you'll see rides on the blimp included in fundraising auctions, and the hangar is often used for toy drives and other community events.

ODDS AND ENDS

Where is the best thrift store?

Have a beer and stay awhile—that's the mindset at Oddballs Nifty Thrift, a nearly 7,000-square-foot thrift and vintage store in Oakland Park. That's because when you walk in, a fridge is stocked with beers, wine, soda, and water to keep you hydrated while hunting through the labyrinth of treasures. And with almost every inch of this place covered with finds, you're going to need it.

Owner Tim Smith opened the store in 2013 in Fort Lauderdale, then relocated to Oakland Park. Today, his parents and best friend help manage Oddballs, greeting everyone who walks through the door and reminding them that everything is on sale (In fact, there's a sign that reads "If you need a discount, just ask. That's how we roll!") One could easily spend hours at Oddballs, sifting through everything from sports memorabilia to vintage clothing, furniture, artwork, glassware, records, magazines and more. Green-thumbed visitors may find something before even stepping inside the store. From the parking lot to the front door you'll walk through a garden of plants, signage, pots, and other decor—and it's all for sale.

ODDBALLS NIFTY THRIFT

WHAT: A nationally ranked thrift store

WHERE: 4281 Dixie Hwy., Oakland Park

COST: Free to enter

PRO TIP: Oddballs neighbors a number of other vintage and second-hand stores on Dixie Highway.

You can't go to Oddballs too often; there's new merchandise coming in every single day.

You never know what you'll find at Oddballs Nifty Thrift.

Relying mostly on word of mouth and social media, Oddballs has become the pinnacle of thrifting in Greater Fort Lauderdale. In fact, it ranked third in the nation on Yelp in 2022 for best vintage and consignment store.

A LEGACY OF CHANGE

Where can you find the gavel that overturned Don't Ask, Don't Tell?

Move over Smithsonian because perhaps the most important museum for LGBTQ history is right here in Fort Lauderdale.

The Stonewall National Museum, Archives & Library (SNMAL) was founded in 1972 by Mark Silber, who started collecting books written on the LGBTQ experience when he was only 17 years old. Today, the museum has grown to include millions of pages of records and memorabilia, including photographs, books, magazines, textiles, pamphlets, protest placards, pins, and artwork. A piece of recent history at SNMAL includes the very gavel used to overturn Don't Ask, Don't Tell in 2010, the decision that allowed LGTBQ people to openly serve in the military. The gavel is on loan to the museum by former US Representative Barney Frank.

Throughout the year, the museum hosts movie screenings, book signings, exhibit openings, and conversations on everything from health to history. In 2024, SNMAL hosted its inaugural Stonewall Uprising reenactment, where the

Top Left: *The Stonewall Museum is a rich resource of books, movies, and music related to the Equality Movement. Photos courtesy Stonewall National Museum Archives and Library*

Top Right: *A display looking at the Disco Era*

Opposite: *A visitor explores an interactive LGBTQ history timeline.*

community was invited to take part in a reenactment of the clash on Christopher Street in 1969 that kickstarted the equality movement. Inside the museum staff even built a replica of the Stonewall Inn, and protesters threw "bricks" and battled with law enforcement after police raided the bar.

Visitors can take part in a guided tour Thursday evenings and Saturday afternoons, as well as by appointment.

STONEWALL NATIONAL MUSEUM, ARCHIVES & LIBRARY

WHAT: The largest collection of LGBTQ history in the world

WHERE: 1300 E Sunrise Blvd., Fort Lauderdale

COST: Free to enter

PRO TIP: SNMAL shares a campus with ArtServe, which houses the World AIDS Museum.

The Stonewall National Women's Fund works to ensure that the stories and contributions of women in the LGBTQ experience is fully explored.

A TREASURE TROVE OF BLACK HISTORY

Where can you find the first edition of *Twelve Years a Slave*?

Fort Lauderdale's black community is embedded in the city's history, and through the efforts of then-county library director Samuel F. Morrison, the sprawling 60,000-square-foot research library opened in 2002. It was only the third of its kind in the entire United States, housing more than 85,000 books, documents, and artifacts telling the story of the Pan African experience. The library also plays host to art exhibits in its 5,000 square foot gallery, lectures in the auditorium, and events like the annual Africana Arts & Humanities Festival.

But the real treasures are stored in the archives, an impressive collection of tens of thousands of books spanning art, music, history, sports, Pan African history, anthropology, fiction, and more. There are also African artworks and treasures like Esther Rolle's Emmy Award for her role in *Summer of My German Soldier*. (Fun fact, Rolle is a Broward County local, born and raised in Pompano Beach). Some other impressive finds include the 1853 first edition of *Twelve Years a Slave*, the personal papers of Roots author Alex Haley, bills of sale from the slave trade, and an emotional emancipation notice of a formerly enslaved woman

AFRICAN AMERICAN RESEARCH LIBRARY AND CULTURAL CENTER

WHAT: See the first edition of *Twelve Years a Slave* and other historical finds.

WHERE: 2650 Sistrunk Blvd., Fort Lauderdale

COST: Free to enter

PRO TIP: Visitors can also go online to see a digital inventory with 2D and 3D scans of the library's collection.

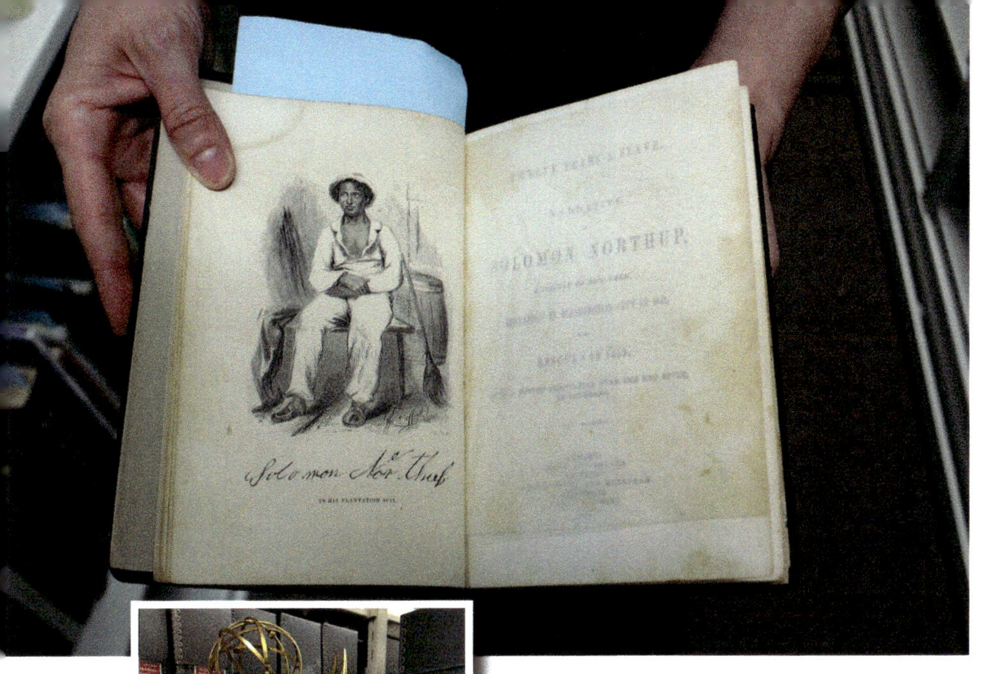

Above: *A first edition of* 12 Years a Slave

Left: *Esther Rolle's Emmy for Outstanding Supporting Actress in* Summer of My German Soldier

in New Orleans looking to buy her children's freedom.

Of this collection, 3,000 of the books came from the private collection of Dr. Dorothy Porter Wesley, a renowned historian and librarian whose life work was preserving the stories and heritage of people of African descent. She served as the librarian at Howard University and also made addendums to the Dewey Decimal System to make it more inclusive of book genres.

The papers of Dr. Niara Sudarkasa, a noted anthropologist and scholar, are stored in the museum's archives. She was born and raised in Fort Lauderdale.

A SCOOP FOR ME, A SCOOP FOR YOU

JAXSON'S ICE CREAM PARLOR

WHAT: Order The Original Kitchen Sink, filled with ice cream and other sweets.

WHERE: 128 S Federal Hwy., Dania Beach

COST: Free to enter

PRO TIP: Don't leave without visiting the country store.

The famous Original Kitchen Sink dessert at Jaxson's

Where can you eat way too much ice cream?

Pulling up to Jaxson's Ice Cream Parlor, don't be surprised to see a line out the door. There are probably families looking for some scoops, a birthday party in progress, an old-school date night over a sundae, or brave foodies looking to order the most iconic item on the menu: The Original Kitchen Sink.

The name is no exaggeration. Served in an actual kitchen sink, the vessel is filled with 1 pound of ice cream per person and topped with bananas, cherries, mixed nuts, and fluffy homemade whipped cream. To up the ante even further, two sparklers are lit as the dessert parades through the dining room before arriving at your table.

Of course, you don't have to commit to a full sink of sugar to enjoy Jaxson's. There are more than 50 different flavors of ice cream as well as old favorites like sundaes, banana splits, shakes, and ice cream soda floats. On the more savory side of the menu, there is a selection of nachos, fries, burgers,

Top Left: *The classic country store sells memorabilia as well as vintage toys.*

Top Right: *You can't miss Jaxson's with its whimsical, circus-like exterior.*

hot dogs, chicken wings, sandwiches, salads, fried shrimp . . . and, believe it or not, even more. This is all served amid the homey Americana decor with walls filled with license plates and road signs, and a charming country store.

Jaxson's has been an institution in Greater Fort Lauderdale since it opened in 1956. It was founded by Monroe Udell, who was known as a man of the community—he openly defied Jim Crow laws of the time and allowed both white and black guests as well as staff in his store; President Barack Obama noted in a radio address how Udell raised the minimum wage of his employees; and for Jaxson's 50th anniversary he raised $30,000 for the Joe DiMaggio Children's Hospital.

When you leave Jaxon's Ice Cream Parlor, both your stomach and your heart will be full.

The restaurant is open late and is close to the airport, making it the perfect stop after landing in Fort Lauderdale.

OPEN SESAME

Psst, how do I get into this speakeasy?

A century after Prohibition, speakeasies have re-emerged on the bar scene—but very few can be considered true speakeasies (having a sign above the door does not a secret bar make).

There are a few speakeasies in Fort Lauderdale, but one we'll blow the lid off of is Room 901 at the Hyatt Centric Las Olas. It's literally located in a hotel room, and guests require a room key and an elevator ride to the ninth floor. With a wave of the room key, the door is unlocked and you step behind black curtains into the dimmed light of the bar decorated with ornate rugs, copper swans, tasseled table lamps, peacock feathers, and velvet seating. At your dinner table, play rounds of dominoes or tic tac toe while waiting for cocktails to be mixed.

It all plays into the spirit of Prohibition, since Broward County was founded back in 1915 when residents wanted to be a dry county, splitting from Dade County to the south. Alcohol sales in the county were legal for the first time when Amendment 18 was repealed in 1933 and the state of Florida allowed counties to decide individually what their rules would be. But let's be honest: There's a reason Fort Lauderdale is nicknamed Fort Liquordale—the area was considered one of the "leakiest" places when it came to Prohibition.

Reservations are required to enter Room 901 (the barkeep needs to know to expect you!) with a two-hour block of time. Play it cool on your way out!

Keep an eye out for the Champagne vending machine on the first floor of the hotel by the elevators.

Room 901 is hidden on the ninth floor of the hotel. Credit Hyatt Centric Las Olas

ROOM 901

WHAT: A speakeasy hidden in a hotel room

WHERE: Hyatt Centric Las Olas, 100 E Las Olas Blvd., Fort Lauderdale

COST: Free entry with a $50 minimum per guest

PRO TIP: Your night doesn't have to end after Room 901; stroll further down Las Olas Boulevard for more bars, restaurants and shops.

IT'S JUST A PARTY, JANET

How do I get the full "Rocky Horror Picture Show" experience?

One of the most enduring historic landmarks in Fort Lauderdale is the Gateway Theater, its vintage marquee announcing its lineup of Hollywood blockbusters, throwback favorites, and independent films.

An ongoing tradition at the theater has been a late-night screening of the 1975 cult classic *The Rocky Horror Picture Show* with a live shadow cast. Before the movie, guests can purchase prop bags filled with everything they'll need to take part in the politically incorrect evening of singalongs, cursing at the screen, and throwing items around the theater. Costumes are highly recommended—especially fishnet stockings. If you need a refresher, *The Rocky Horror Picture Show* is a musical comedy about a young couple whose car breaks down. They head to the castle of Dr. Frank N. Furter, who is in the middle of hosting a costume party; hilarity ensues.

The Gateway's first film screening was *Up Front* back in 1951, and it also hosted the premiere of *Where the Boys Are*

GATEWAY THEATER

WHAT: Watch *The Rocky Horror Picture Show* with a shadow cast.

WHERE: 1820 E Sunrise Blvd., Fort Lauderdale

COST: Ticket prices vary.

PRO TIP: Tickets are only $6 on Tuesdays.

Savor Cinema in Fort Lauderdale also hosts its own screenings of the movie with a shadow cast.

For years, the Gateway Theater has hosted shadow casts for an interactive screening of Rocky Horror Picture Show.

in 1960, the film that put Fort Lauderdale on the map as a spring break hotspot. Owners have come and gone over the years, but this independent movie theatre has held a special place in local cinephiles' hearts. Ticket prices are always low, and popcorn is always drizzled in real butter.

THE STORY OF RUBIN STACY

Why is Davie Boulevard also called Rubin Stacy Memorial Boulevard?

A new street sign went up in 2022 marking Rubin Stacy Memorial Boulevard—and for many it was an unknown name. But his descendants hope the sign will help spread the word of the victim of Fort Lauderdale's only lynching.

In 1935—when Jim Crow Laws were in full effect in Florida—Rubin Stacy allegedly knocked on the door of Mrs. J. L. Jones. The encounter ended with him running from her home and getting caught in her laundry line; the stories vary of what happened. Some say he was asking for a glass of water, others say he was looking for work, but it ended with her claiming he tried to attack her with a knife.

Three days later, Stacy was caught and the sheriff's office was driving him to Miami to be jailed when a mob managed to pull him out of the car, take him back to the scene of the alleged crime, and hung him with the laundry line he had

RUBIN STACY MEMORIAL BOULEVARD

WHAT: A reminder of the darker moments in our past

WHERE: Davie Boulevard in Fort Lauderdale

COST: Free to enter

PRO TIP: The black cemetery where Rubin Stacy was buried in an unmarked grave was razed to build I-95; it's believed he and others are under the Sunrise Boulevard exit.

Rubin Stacy is included in the National Memorial for Peace and Justice in Montgomery, Alabama which memorializes victims of lynching.

A portion of Davie Boulevard in Fort Lauderdale was named Rubin Stacy Memorial Boulevard to honor the only man recorded to be lynched in Broward County.

tripped over a few days before. His hands were still cuffed. Thousands came out to watch, some cut pieces of his overalls as souvenirs, photos were taken, and when he was cut down, there were 17 bullet holes in his body. The story went national, with photos of his lifeless body published in local and national newspapers.

The area where Stacy was murdered is located on the 3100 block of Davie Boulevard, and while there is no memorial marker, in 2022 the city added Rubin Stacy Memorial Highway to a 2-mile stretch of Davie. His family told the local news that they hope when people see the sign, they'll google Stacy's name.

PAINTING REALITY

Where can you see a Frida Kahlo original?

Frida Kahlo has a spot in the upper echelons of the art world, recognized for her self portraits, bright colors, and for putting Mexican artwork on the global stage. Her pieces can be seen in museums in Mexico City, Paris, New York City, Washington, DC—and Fort Lauderdale.

Autorretrato en una página del diario (Self-portrait on Diary Page) is a part of NSU Art Museum Fort Lauderdale's permanent collection; it's an impressive get, considering there are only about 150 pieces of her work in existence (depending on who you ask). The piece is a self portrait from her diary, using watercolor, crayon, pencil, and ink, a more surrealist take on her self portraits. It shows her side profile with a floating hand holding onto her left ear. Below is simply the location and year it was painted, Coyoacán 1945, and her name.

NSU Art Museum Fort Lauderdale has a large collection of Latin American art, and the Kahlo piece, along with more

NSU ART MUSEUM FORT LAUDERDALE

WHAT: Home to a Frida Kahlo self portrait

WHERE: One E Las Olas Blvd., Fort Lauderdale

COST: Fees apply for admission, with discounts for seniors, military, certain ages, and students.

PRO TIP: The first Thursday of the month is Sunny Days and Starry Nights at the museum, meaning free entry for all as well as two-for-one all-day happy hour.

Christo and Jeanne-Claude's *Surrounded Islands* documentation exhibition is on permanent display here; the two covered an island in Biscayne Bay in pink fabric in 1983.

The exterior of the NSU Art Museum Fort Lauderdale is "Acid Free" by Jen Stark. Courtesy of Steven Brooke

than 70 other paintings, were donated by Stanley and Pearl Goodman, longtime collectors of Latin American art. With the donation, the museum launched the Stanley and Pearl Goodman Center for the Study of Latin American Art. *Autorretrato en una página del diario* has been included in a number of exhibits at the museum, including "I Paint My Reality," inspired by a quote from Kahlo about how she does not paint dreams.

SOMETHING FISHY

What shape is the Pompano pier?

Jutting out into the Atlantic Ocean in Pompano Beach is a nearly 900-foot pier with blue sails overhead protecting visitors and fishers from the Florida sun.

There are plenty of design Easter eggs throughout the pier—the black-and-white photo of the original pier when it was built in 1963, paintings of marine life that can be found in these waters, and pavers that glow in the dark when the sun sets. The most fun feature, though, can only be seen from up high: the pier is in the shape of a pompano fish. From the air, one can see that at the end of the pier is the oblong face of a fish with a mouth as well as an eye.

The pier originally opened in 1963, transforming the beachfront into a gathering place for fishermen, swimmers, and beachgoers. Hurricanes did their damage to the pier over the years, and in 2022 the city unveiled its brand-new pier and fishing village. The pier is twice as wide now and is higher to accommodate sea level rise, and graceful white sails overhead protect sightseers from the sun as they relax on a bench. For fishermen, the Bait Shack offers a fishing package that includes a rod, gear, bait, bucket, knife, one-day fishing license, and parking validation at the pier garage.

POMPANO BEACH FISHER FAMILY PIER

WHAT: Walk a fishing pier in the shape of a pompano.

WHERE: 222 N Pompano Beach Blvd.

COST: Sightseeing is free, and daily fishing permits are available at resident and nonresident rates.

PRO TIP: There are three other piers in Broward County—Dania Beach, Lauderale-by-the-Sea, and Deerfield Beach. Pompano and Deerfield both have public underwater cameras so you can watch marine life!

Above: *The pier at Pompano Beach is in the shape of a pompano fish, with its eyeball serving as a fishing hole. Photos courtesy City of Pompano Beach*

Left: *The Fisher Family Pier in Pompano Beach*

A fun place to fish is at the round cutout at the end of the pier, the fish eye. Watch out for hungry pelicans when you gut your catch!

The parking garage for the pier is covered in murals, including *Reef Life* by Taylor Smith (Dreamweaver) and *A Place I'd Rather Be* by Mike and Donna-Lee Savlen.

JOYSTICK HERO

Where can I resurrect my Mortal Kombat moves?

Millennials, Gen X, and those yearning for nostalgia from decades past will feel right at home at Glitch Bar, a bar that will take you back to the days you blew your allowance at the arcade.

Inside, the dark bar is illuminated with black lights to showcase band posters and beer pulls hanging like bats from the ceiling, rows of action figures at command, skateboard decks as decor, and a DJ booth covered with cassettes and VHS tapes. Order from your choice of more than two dozen beers, a selection of cocktails (the Cherry Bomb is a fun one, garnished with a red, white, and blue popsicle), and light bites. Throughout the week, there are specials and DJ nights spinning music ranging from hard rock to '90s, synth rock, and other throwback jams.

GLITCH BAR

WHAT: A bar with plenty of throw-back arcade games

WHERE: 905 NE Fifth Ave., Fort Lauderdale

COST: You can either pay a small entry fee or purchase a drink to enter the arcade.

PRO TIP: Glitch is located in the buzzing MASS District, with neighbors like Italian restaurant Heritage, Blueprint Cookies, and Karma Kava.

That's just the bar area, though, and those who come to Glitch are here for what's beyond the velvet rope. For $10 (or the purchase of a drink) gamers will receive a wristband that grants them access to a world of arcade games from yesteryear and today. From Atari to Street Fighter and Teenage Mutant Ninja Turtles to Contra, Neo Geo, Pac Man, and Mortal Kombat, no tokens are needed to defeat the boss. The arcades are spread throughout three rooms, and each machine is outfitted with a handy cup holder for your drink. The bar is the only location in South Florida with a Killer Queen Draft League, with monthly tournaments hosted at Glitch (participants get free pizza!).

Top Left: *Rack up points while playing Skee-Ball.*

Top Right: *Glitch has plenty of old-school arcade games, including Mortal Kombat and Street Fighter.*

While the bar is 21 and older, parents wanting to introduce youngsters to their childhood games can bring their kids to Glitch on Sundays until 8 p.m. with an adult (with the purchase of a wristband).

There is a slew of Florida beers on tap, including suds from Suncreek Brewery, Tripping Animals Crewing Co., Sun Lab Brewing, and 26 Degree Brewing.

BOOK WORMS

Where can I be transported to a Victorian library?

If you're a bookworm, then for you, paradise looks like the Old Florida Book Shop. Filled with books spanning centuries and covering the walls from floor to ceiling, owner William Chrisant's used bookstore houses all genres, from nonfiction and science to poetry, LGBTQ literature, mysticism, novels, and children's reads. And if you show up when the store isn't open, the shelves outside have books for sale for just $1; through the honor system, simply choose your books and drop the appropriate number of dollar bills through the mail slot.

Chrisant opened the store in 2011 (he's also owned bookstores in Philadelphia and Cleveland) and had the 16-foot-tall bookshelves custom made to fill with books for just about every reader, with rolling ladders for those hard-to-reach shelves. With the sounds of classical music in the background, visitors can spend hours poring over lithographs, signed books, maps dating back to the 16th century, vintage magazines, sculptures, leather-bound series tucked away in glass cases, and even a megalodon tooth and a Sumerian cuneiform tablet from 2300 BCE.

And what's a bookstore without a furry friend? One of the most popular staff members at the Old Florida Book Shop is Peter the cat, a gray tabby who naps in the bookshelves or stretches out on the oriental rugs for belly rubs.

OLD FLORIDA BOOK SHOP

WHAT: Your dream bookstore with antiquities and oddities

WHERE: 3426 Griffin Rd., Fort Lauderdale

COST: Free to enter

PRO TIP: The oldest book in the owner's collection is an edition of Plutarch's *Lives of the Noble Grecians and Romans* published in 1480.

Top Left: *The books at the Old Florida Book Shop span genres and centuries.*

Top Right: *A customer reaches for a book.*

Left: *Peter the cat is an attraction all on his own at the bookstore.*

Ask Chrisant to see the paperwork signed by Amelia Earhart, which is hung at the bookstore.

167 STEPS TO THE TOP

When can I climb the lighthouse?

Driving down A1A at night, drivers are treated to a vintage light show at the Hillsboro Point Lighthouse while passing through Hillsboro Point.

Once a month the public can get up close and personal with the lighthouse when it's open for tours. Take a 20-minute boat shuttle landing at the lighthouse and climb up the 167 steps in a winding staircase to the top. From here, there are impeccable views of the Hillsboro Inlet as it joins the Atlantic Ocean. Boats make a day out of the lighthouse being open and children play on the shore. Out on the ocean, keep an eye out for sharks and other marine life. When you get back to the bottom, take a photo with your certificate proudly announcing, "I survived the climb!"

HILLSBORO POINT LIGHTHOUSE

WHAT: Climb 167 steps for pristine ocean views.

WHERE: 907 Hillsboro Mile, Hillsboro Beach

COST: A yearly pass is available for purchase.

PRO TIP: Bring closed-toe shoes; otherwise, choose from a pile of Crocs to make the climb.

The lighthouse has been a fixture since it opened in 1907, guiding ships to shore. It was built in Detroit in 1906, and it was shipped from Lake Erie to Lake Michigan, down the Mississippi River, through the Gulf of Mexico, around Key West, and then north to the inlet to reach its final home. As for the Fresnel lens, it came all the way from Paris. Many Barefoot Mailmen passed by the lighthouse on their journey to deliver

---

There are three webcams set up at the lighthouse, so visitors can check out the views from the comfort of their home, too.

Top: *There are 167 steps to the top of the lighthouse.*

Left: The Hillsboro Lighthouse was erected in 1907 and is still functional.

mail, and a statue in their honor was erected nearby. While you wait your turn to climb to the top, volunteers share stories about the mailmen and the keepers who kept the lighthouse going.

More than a century later, the lighthouse is now fully automated, but it's still a majestic sight at night, the lens spinning and illuminating the beach.

PSST PSST PSST

Where can I play with cats while enjoying a cup of coffee?

One cat is snoozing on the couch while two others chase dragonflies hanging from a wand, and another is hiding under a bench, still unsure of her surroundings. All of them, though, are looking for their forever homes. The Good Luck Cat Cafe takes in about a dozen kittens and cats at a time, and the public is invited to come hang out with them. This gives the cats the chance for socialization, and hopefully, someone will come and fall in love.

The cafe started in 2016 as a collaboration between two local pet rescues, Lady Luck Animal Rescue and Good Karma. Their names combined for the name of the café, and today Lady Luck manages the cafe in Flagler Village. Inside, volunteers sell drinks from a mini fridge or can prepare a fresh cup of coffee; there are also pre-packaged snacks that guests can nibble on. Since the Good Luck Cat Cafe opened its doors to feline friends, more than 400 cats have been adopted.

GOOD LUCK CAT CAFE

WHAT: A place to play with cats looking for their forever homes

WHERE: 901 Progresso Dr. #202, Fort Lauderdale

COST: A donation in the amount of your choice for entry

PRO TIP: Why not host a birthday party at the café, giving the cats some TLC while also raising money for the rescue?

Each day, Lady Luck Animal Rescue receives around 20 calls from good Samaritans who have found cats.

The kitties all have different personalities and stories of how they wound up at the cat cafe. Some were wandering the streets alone, and others were removed from abusive homes.

Cat lovers can pop by with a donation of any amount to play with the cats, and they can also volunteer their time and share the word on social media. Donations go toward cat food and supplies, and rent for the cafe. The ultimate win, though, would be a cat finding a home.

Top: *A cat takes a break from the exercise wheel.*

Left: *There are plenty of cozy spots for a cat nap.*

O, CHRISTMAS TREE

Where can I get in the holiday spirit 365 days a year?

December 26 means nothing around here, because at The Christmas Palace, Yule is a season that runs all year long.

At more than 20,000 square feet, the Fort Lauderdale store is a maze of holiday fun. Each room is filled with floor-to-ceiling Christmas trees decorated in ornaments with different themes, from girly Candyland to glitzy silver baubles or more rustic wooden snowflakes. And because it's Florida, there is also a tree decked out with flamingos, shells, coral, seahorses, and a Santa merman. The shelves are covered with candles, ornaments, and wall decor, and on the floor there's life-sized reindeer, nutcrackers, soldiers, snowmen, and everything else you need to be extra for the holiday season. There are also alcoves with specialty items, including a room dedicated to full sets and pieces for nativity scenes, as well as angels for tree toppers and decor.

Over-the-top decorators will swoon over the selections of glass ball ornaments, lined up in a rainbow and including all shades from red to violet, as well as silver and gold. There's also a floral room, with faux greenery needed for wreaths and mantles. And don't forget to take a stroll down Glitterville, which lives up to its name with plenty of sparkly decor. Tablescapes will never be barren, thanks to the tablecloths, napkins, and centerpieces.

The Christmas Palace has been a Fort Lauderdale mainstay since 1994 and is owned by Jimmy Knips and his family. They consider the store a happy place, where they welcome people to

---

There is another Christmas Palace location in Hialeah Gardens, about 45 minutes southwest of Fort Lauderdale.

walk around or take photos to lighten the mood, if that's what they need. And with the change in technology and trends, year over year they've updated their inventory. For the Christmas fanatic, that's a welcome option—the Knips family has customers who keep their trees up all year long and decorate for St. Patrick's Day, Easter, the Fourth of July, Halloween, and more.

THE CHRISTMAS PALACE

WHAT: A yearlong Christmas shop

WHERE: 200 E Sunrise Blvd., Fort Lauderdale

COST: Free to enter

PRO TIP: Can't make it to the store? The Christmas Palace has an e-commerce business, too.

The Christmas Palace is filled with ornaments, tree decor, lawn fixtures, and anything else you need to celebrate the season.

CULTURAL REUNION

When is the annual Seminole powwow?

With the light dimmed in the ballroom of the Seminole Hard Rock Hotel & Casino, the audience awaits the beginning of the Grand Entry, kicking off the annual Seminole Tribal Fair and Powwow.

Each year, members of the Seminole Tribe and beyond descend upon Greater Fort Lauderdale for a long weekend celebration. It's a tradition that has been going on for more than 50 years, bringing together dancers, drummers, artisans, filmmakers, animal enthusiasts, and the general public. Starting with the welcome ceremony, men, women, and children in their regalia dance in the ballroom and also welcome the arrival of pageant royalty, elected officials, members of the military, and other dignitaries. Even the youngest dancers take part, following their parents and grandparents—a new generation absorbing the elements of their culture and community.

SEMINOLE TRIBAL FAIR AND POWWOW

WHAT: An annual celebration of Seminole culture

WHERE: Seminole Hard Rock Hotel & Casino Hollywood, 1 Seminole Way, Davie

COST: Free to enter

PRO TIP: Vendors include artisans from tribes across the country.

All are welcome as spectators of the powwow and other festivities, watching contestants in dance categories and drumming groups as well as a fashion show, the Native Reel

---

To learn more about Seminole culture, visit the Ah-Tah-Thi-Ki Museum at the Big Cypress Seminole Indian Reservation.

Dancers line up in their regalia for the grand entry. Photo courtesy Seminole Tribune

Cinema Festival, wildlife shows, and a vendor fair with Seminole ribbon skirts, beaded and metal jewelry, woven items, and other artisan wares. The tribal fair and powwow weekend culminates in a concert from the headlining band; past performers have included Sublime, the Frontmen, and Bret Michaels.

The Tribal Fair and Powwow has been a tradition in the area for more than 50 years, not only bringing together tribal members within Florida but Seminole people in other states.

COWBOY TOWN

Where can you see a buckin' bronco?

For most people, Florida conjures images of idyllic beaches and prehistoric alligators. But the Sunshine State has a history of cowboys and rodeo culture; in fact, Florida sells more than $500 million in cattle and calves each year.

West of Fort Lauderdale is the town of Davie, also known as "Cowboy Town." Here rodeos are scheduled multiple times a year at the Bergeron Rodeo Grounds. It's located in the town's Western-themed downtown and includes a 72,000-square-foot arena that seats 5,500 people—more than 30,000 people a year come out to watch the high-octane excitement of bull rides, calf-roping, and bucking broncos. In 2024, *USA Today* ranked Weekley Brothers Davie Pro Rodeo as the No. 3 rodeo in the country.

Each rodeo kicks off with a flurry of flags carried out by cowboys and cowgirls, then contestants from around the country vie to be the best in their category. The first rodeo was hosted in the town in 1946, and in 1986 the Weekley and Parrish families teamed up to host Professional Rodeo Cowboys Association–sanctioned rodeos. Today, there are youth and adult rodeo competitions, including the Orange Blossom Festival Rodeo and the highly anticipated Southeastern Circuit Finals Rodeo, sponsored by the Seminole Tribe of Florida.

Besides the action in the arena there are food trucks, cold beer, a petting zoo, and vendors selling cowboy hats and western-themed purses, clothing, drinkware, and more.

We'll tip our hat to that.

The first rodeo on the grounds was hosted in 1946, back when the stadium was called the Davie Rodeo Arena.

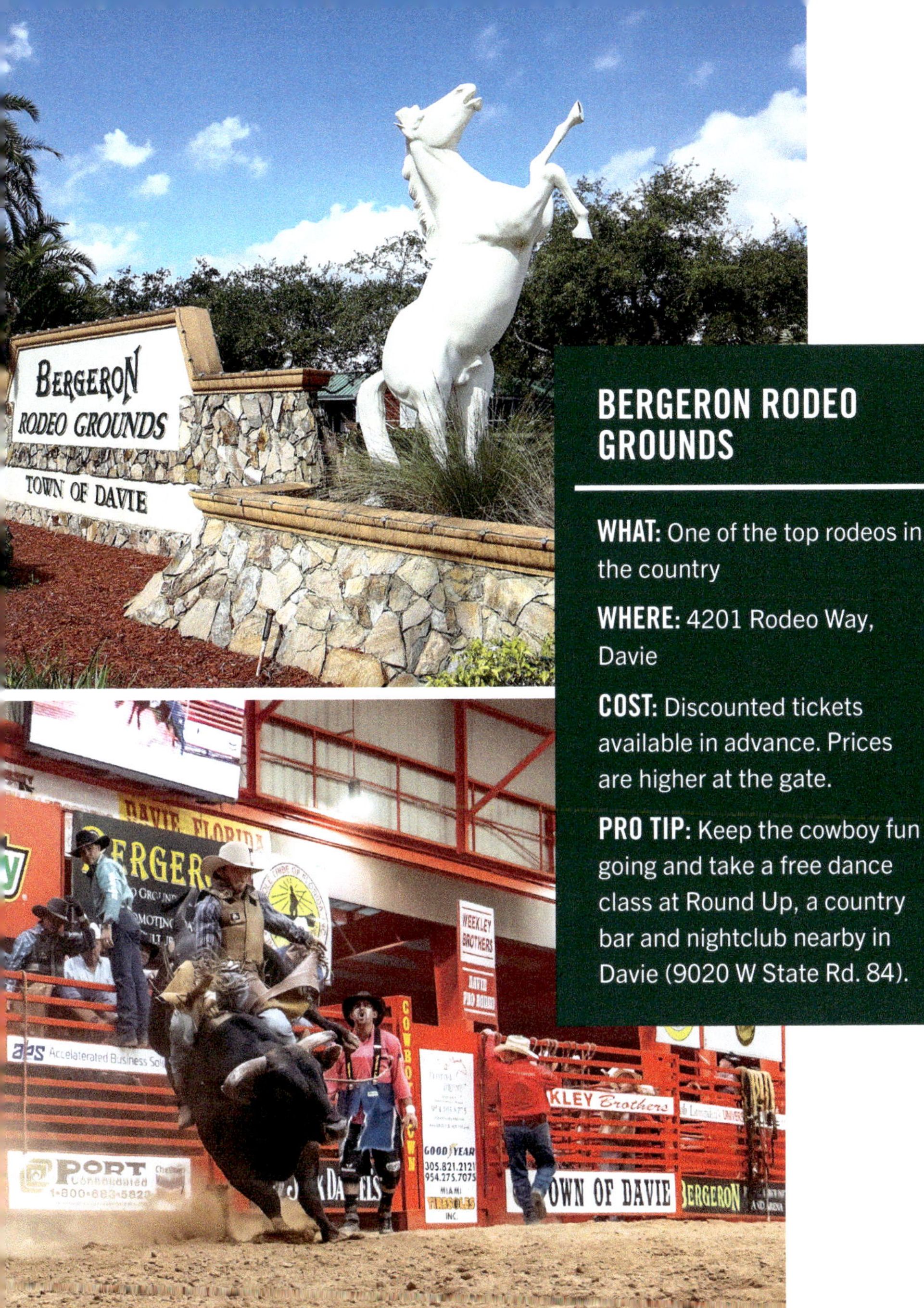

BERGERON RODEO GROUNDS

WHAT: One of the top rodeos in the country

WHERE: 4201 Rodeo Way, Davie

COST: Discounted tickets available in advance. Prices are higher at the gate.

PRO TIP: Keep the cowboy fun going and take a free dance class at Round Up, a country bar and nightclub nearby in Davie (9020 W State Rd. 84).

Top: *The entry to the Bergeron Rodeo Grounds. Courtesy Jillian Cain Photography / Shutterstock.com*

Bottom: *The crowd watches a bull rider during a rodeo at the Bergeron Rodeo Grounds. Courtesy T.J. Hunt Photography*

GO WITH THE FLO

Where can I get breakfast 24 hours a day?

On buzzing Las Olas Boulevard in downtown Fort Lauderdale is a restaurant that has stood the test of time, watching the city grow from a small beach town to a major tourist destination. It's The Floridian, recognizable for its bold black and yellow exterior and the fact that it's been there longer than almost any other business on the thoroughfare.

Open since 1937, the 24-hour diner is all about tradition and a good ol' American breakfast you can order at any time of day, any day of the week. On the menu, expect to find breakfast favorites like eggs benedict, smoked salmon and eggs, and pancakes, as well as dozens of burger and sandwich options (including the Floridian sandwich, grilled tuna salad, and Swiss on rye with bacon and tomato). And since you can have brunch any time you like, there are mimosas, Kir royale, poinsettias, and bellinis, too. For years, customers could get a chuckle from the Fat Cat breakfast on the menu—a $500 order that consisted of a bottle of Dom Perignon, New York strip steak, two eggs, home fries or grits, and your choice of toast or a biscuit.

All of this is served in a cozy setting oozing with nostalgia, with walls covered in hundreds of framed photographs of

THE FLORIDIAN

WHAT: Pop some champagne with your breakfast.

WHERE: 1492 E Las Olas Blvd., Fort Lauderdale

COST: Free to enter

PRO TIP: Happy Hour is Monday through Friday from 3 to 7 p.m.

For a sip of Florida, order a glass of freshly squeezed orange juice (the press is right on the counter of the bar).

Left: *The Floridian is a blast from the past, from its black-and-white penny tile to vintage signage.*

Right: *The walls of the Floridian are covered with vintage memorabilia.*

stars and signage from around town. Hanging from the ceiling are chandeliers and Tiffany-style stained glass lamps, and perhaps a Coca Cola fixture or two.

Longtime owner Butch Samp, whom the *Sun Sentinel* declared Fort Lauderdale's unofficial mayor, died in 2023 and the future of The Flo was in limbo. But it wasn't the end of an era, as locals feared. New owners purchased the diner and vowed to stay true to the legacy of the eatery.

HIGH DIVE

Where can I dive into a pool from dizzying heights?

Whether you're waiting for the Water Taxi at stop 6 or boating through the New River, a sight that can't be ignored is the soaring Dive Tower at the Fort Lauderdale Aquatic Center. Coming in at a whopping 27 meters tall (that's 162 steps to the top), the new age–style dive tower also has high-dive levels at 15, 20, and 24 meters for some of the best divers out there. For those of us who prefer to stay closer to the Earth, there are one- to 10-meter diving platforms.

Swimmers and divers have descended on Fort Lauderdale for nearly a century, going back to when the city's Casino Pool opened in 1928 and hosted swimmers who needed a place to practice without freezing their swim caps. It was the first Olympic-sized pool (that's 50 meters by 20 meters) to be built in the state of Florida. Sunny Fort Lauderdale made an impression on its aquatic visitors, and students told their friends all about it when they returned home. From there, Spring Break mania ensued and continues to this day.

DIVE TOWER

WHAT: A 27-meter-tall dive tower

WHERE: Fort Lauderdale Aquatic Center, 501 Seabreeze Blvd., Fort Lauderdale

COST: There is a small fee for passes.

PRO TIP: In order to go above five meters on the diving board, special training and safety certifications are required.

Swimming was all the rage in American sports during this time, leading to cities vying to be the host of the International Swimming Hall of Fame. Fort Lauderdale won over Houston, Texas, and Louisville, Kentucky, and during the 1965 ribbon-cutting, celebrities in attendance included Duke Kahanamoku (considered the father of modern surfing), Jackie Gleason, Ted Williams, Eleanor Holm, Buster Crabbe, Esther Williams,

Above: *The Casino Pool, the first Olympic-sized pool in Florida. Courtesy History Fort Lauderdale*

Left: *The tallest diving board at the Aquatic Center is 24 meters. Courtesy City of Fort Lauderdale*

and Johnny Weissmuller (an Olympic swimmer and the star of "Tarzan"). Gold medalist Donna de Varona was pulled in on a surfboard, a crown atop her head.

Today, the Diving Tower is a part of a major overhaul at the Aquatic Center and the International Swimming Hall of Fame. Soon visitors will be able to see everything from "Tarzan" memorabilia to Olympic medals and swimming artifacts from ancient times.

If the high dive isn't your thing, check out the hours throughout the week for lap times in the pool.

MOUNT TRASHMORE

Where did they film the Hollywood sign?

Florida isn't exactly known for its high elevation—South Florida in particular. In fact, Fort Lauderdale's elevation is about nine feet above sea level. So where does a movie director find a mountain for their next Hollywood film?

A landfill, of course. In 2011, locals were turning their heads when they saw 20-foot-high, white letters spelling out "Hollywood" at the Monarch Hill Renewable Energy Park (or, as locals call it, Mount Trashmore). Soon it hit the news that the landfill was going to be a stand-in for the Hollywood Hills in the Tom Cruise movie *Rock of Ages*, which was filmed throughout Greater Fort Lauderdale (including Revolution Live downtown, which doubled as the Bourbon Room). Waste Management received a usage fee from the movie, and it was donated as scholarships to four students at Monarch High School in Coconut Creek.

Monarch Hill Renewable Energy Park has been a part of the landscape since it opened in 1965, spread over 500 acres in unincorporated Broward County—it's a sort of Bermuda Triangle where Deerfield Beach, Pompano Beach, and Coconut

MONARCH HILL RENEWABLE ENERGY PARK

WHAT: A landfill turned Hollywood backdrop

WHERE: 2700 Wiles Rd., Pompano Beach

COST: Free to enter

PRO TIP: While the landfill is not open to the public, it's easy to see from the roads in the area.

Monarch Hill Renewable Energy Park is a fitting name, as neighboring Coconut Creek is the butterfly capital of the world.

Crew from Waste Management, Visit Lauderdale, the film studio, and four scholarship winners in front of the "Hollywood sign." Courtesy Waste Management

Creek intersect. Waste Management's green-and-yellow trucks are also a fixture in the community, winding through neighborhoods on trash collection days.

And of course, part of a totally rad LA landmark.

ON THE SHOULDERS OF GIANTS

What is the wood carving at D.C. Alexander Park?

D.C. Alexander Park has been a draw for locals and visitors ever since it underwent a major renovation, adding a playground, landscaping, and an architectural overlook. But one thing that has stayed the same is a 20-foot-tall cypress wood carving, a fixture since 1983.

The piece, *Trail of the Whispering Giants #43*, was created by artist Peter "Wolf" Toth and is a part of a series of 74 carvings he completed across the United States and Canada to honor indigenous people.

Then-Fort Lauderdale Commissioner Virginia Young, who was an advocate for bringing the piece to the city, told the *Sun Sentinel*, "I'm interested in the future and afraid that nobody will remember that's how South Florida started." She had lived in Fort Lauderdale since 1928, overlapping with the Stranahans, the founders of the city who had a trading post in the city and a positive rapport with the Seminoles.

Toth confers with local indigenous communities while working on the statues, and the piece is always donated to the community it is displayed in. He was reportedly adopted into the Eastern Band of Cherokee Indians. Born in Hungary but raised in the United States, Toth told the *Sun Sentinel* in 1991, "My people were refugees in our own country. Native Americans are also refugees in their own land."

The park is named after David Clifford "D.C." Alexander, a beach developer who donated the land to the city.

Trail of the Whispering Giants *at D.C. Alexander Park. Courtesy Jillian Cain / Stock.Adobe.com*

D.C. ALEXANDER PARK

WHAT: Home of *Trail of the Whispering Giants #43*

WHERE: 500 Seabreeze Blvd., Fort Lauderdale

COST: Free to enter

PRO TIP: The piece at D.C. Alexander Park isn't the only one in Florida; while there isn't an official list of the giants and their locations, there is a carving in Punta Gorda, and an early piece made in DeLand was lost to rot.

STARGAZING

Where can I see the planets and the stars?

After dark, Markham Park in Sunrise draws a whole new crowd of visitors—astrophiles (a fancy name for those who love the sky, the moon, stars, galaxies, and planets). At the Fox Observatory they can get up close and personal with the night sky.

The observatory is managed by the South Florida Amateur Astronomers Association (SFAAA), a group of astronomy enthusiasts founded in 1965. Every Saturday, the public is invited to join them at sundown as they open the retracting roof of the observatory to gaze through two telescopes. Depending on the time of the year, it might be the bright planet of Venus or Saturn with its rings. Jupiter makes an appearance with its 97 moons, and then there's the rusty spot of Mars. For the SFAAA, the best part is introducing astronomy to people young and old and seeing them awestruct when they see a planet, the moon, or constellations up close for the first time. Hundreds of budding astronomers come by each week; the club's favorite exclamations: "Is that real?" and "Oh, wow!"

FOX OBSERVATORY

WHAT: Get up close with the night sky every Saturday.

WHERE: Markham Park, 16001 W State Rd. 84, Sunrise

COST: Free to enter, donations welcome

PRO TIP: Take a moment to admire the circle drive in front of the observatory, with a sun dial surrounded by symbols of the planets and zodiac signs.

Visitors to Markham Park can also take part in archery, disc golf, the remote-controlled airfield, and an outdoor shooting range.

Above: *"Oh traveler observe here the swift passage of time and reflect upon the day and your good use of it."—Anonymous*

Left: *The symbol of Aquarius outside of the Fox Observatory*

Fox Observatory is named for Dr. Joseph Dennison Fox, a professor of astronomy and an early member of the SFAAA. He donated his six-inch refracting telescope to the club, a piece that is more than 100 years old. The observatory was founded in 1977, and in the mid 2020s a couple donated their 14-inch reflecting telescope to the club. Now visitors can use old and new technology to take in the beauty of the night sky.

CHOO, CHOO

Where can I ride on a miniature train?

You can get around town by riding on the Tri-Rail and the Brightline trains, and the Florida East Coast Railway cuts through Greater Fort Lauderdale on a regular basis. But perhaps the most interesting—and smallest—rides of them all are the trains that weave their way through Tradewinds Park in Coconut Creek.

On the third Saturday and Sunday of the month from 10 a.m. to 4 p.m., volunteers from the Tradewinds & Atlantic Railroad give rides to the public on model trains, picking up passengers at the Goodwin Train Station overlooking Lake Sorenson, then winding through the tracks passing a barn, going

TRADEWINDS PARK

WHAT: Hop aboard a miniature locomotive.

WHERE: 3600 W Sample Rd., Coconut Creek

COST: There is a small fee per car to enter the park. The train rides are also available at a small fee.

PRO TIP: Riders must be able to walk to the track on their own (no infants, sorry) and pregnant women are unable to ride on the trains.

Volunteers from the Tradewinds & Atlantic Railroad Inc. host train rides at Tradewinds Park one weekend a month. Photos courtesy Tradewinds & Atlantic Railroad Inc.

through the "Unnel" (not a tunnel!), and going over Archer's Crossing and other sights. The group of hobbyists manage and maintain the tracks and are there to educate the hundreds of visitors who come out for the unique experience, from little ones exploring trains for the first time to hobbyists and adults indulging in a little nostalgia. Many locals remember spending time at Tradewinds Park, whether it was a birthday party or field trip to ride the ponies or hop aboard the miniature trains.

Tradewinds & Atlantic Railroad Inc. was founded in 1972 as the Florida Live Steamers–Southern Division, and the tracks were completed at the park in 1990. The trains are a combination of diesel and steam engines and are one-eighth of the size of a real train. That's 11 times the size of a toy train! And by the way, the volunteers bring those out, too, for sale and to instill a love of locomotives in their young visitors.

During the holidays, don't be surprised if you see Santa Claus riding on the tracks.

FROM RUM RUNNERS TO KAYAKERS

How did Whiskey Creek get its name?

Whiskey Creek in Hollywood is known as one of the go-to parks for paddleboarding, kayaking, fishing, and boating. It's a serene place to experience Florida's natural state. It didn't always have that reputation, though. For instance, it got its name because it served as a popular route for bootleggers in the 1920s and '30s.

Rum runners would pick up bottles of liquor in the Bahamas, turn back around to Florida, and mark up each bottle three or four times for a hefty profit. Whiskey Creek was the ideal route to take because of its isolation and shallow waters, meaning the Coast Guard probably wasn't traversing the waterways in their larger vessels. Instead, bootleggers could hide in the canopy of the mangroves. However, word would eventually spread, and other criminals would hide out to hijack and rob the rum runners.

WHISKEY CREEK HIDEOUT

WHAT: A state park with a criminal past

WHERE: 6503 N Ocean Dr., Dania Beach

COST: There is a fee for parking.

PRO TIP: Stop by the Waterfront Bar & Eatery inside the park to refuel.

Other crimes are associated with Whiskey Creek. In 1967, the bodies of two women were found weighted down in the creek. Two men were arrested, including burglar and surfing star John "Murph the Surf" Roland. Three years earlier, he burglarized the American Museum of Natural History in New York in what was considered the "Jewel Heist of the Century." Roland notoriously turned his life around, though; when he was released from prison in 1986, he became an ordained

Once a thoroughfare for rum runners, Whiskey Creek is now for kayaking, paddleboarding, and other outdoor adventures. Courtesy Matt Tilghman / Shutterstock.com

minister and a public speaker, and he served as a chaplain for inmates. He died in 2020.

Whiskey Creek is located within Dr. Von D. Mizell-Eula Johnson State Park in honor of the leaders of the movement to desegregate Fort Lauderdale's beaches. The park was originally the "colored beach," and Mizell and Johnson were also instrumental in turning it into a state park in 1973.

Experience Whiskey Creek with a helpful guide by taking part in the park's eco tours and sunset tours by kayak or paddleboard.

VENICE OF AMERICA

Where can you experience a bit of Italy in Fort Lauderdale?

Fort Lauderdale has a few nicknames, but perhaps the most refined is the Venice of America. That's thanks to the 300 miles of waterways that wind through the city, from canals to the Intracoastal Waterway.

It only makes sense, then, that one can hitch a ride on a gondola for a romantic excursion on the water. Las Olas Gondola has been providing rides to locals and visitors to Fort Lauderdale, a part of engagements, anniversaries, and parties, or just serving those who want to tour the city from a unique vantage point. Guests hop aboard the Romantic Venice for a 75-minute ride, with the gondolier (each is a licensed captain) in their dapper striped outfit working at the stern while riders enjoy the experience from a private cabin. You're welcome

Other unique ways to explore the waterways is Cruisin' Tikis, Riverfront Gondola Tours, and the Water Taxi.

Explore Fort Lauderdale from the comfort of a romantic gondola. Photos courtesy Martha Beachem

LAS OLAS GONDOLA

WHAT: A unique gondola ride through Fort Lauderdale

WHERE: Meet at the Las Olas River House, 333 Las Olas Way, Fort Lauderdale

COST: Prices vary depending on the number of people and time of the cruise. Call to get specific pricing.

PRO TIP: There are plenty of restaurants in the area to purchase food from to enjoy on the gondola ride.

to bring your own food and drink, and if you're feeling extra romantic, the company can provide a message in a bottle for an extra fee.

Las Olas Gondola offers daytime, full moon, sunset, and nighttime cruises, with sunset being the most popular. Whatever time you choose, cruising down the Intracoastal makes for a fun sightseeing tour with the massive yachts and multi-million-dollar waterfront homes. Whether you can afford them or not, it's fun to at least play pretend by choosing your favorites.

REMEMBER ME

What are those giant skeletons for?

Sugar skulls, bright yellow marigolds, and giant skeletons—it's the Day of the Dead in Fort Lauderdale.

Inspired by the Mexican holiday Día de los Muertos, the festival is a way to pay tribute to the dead. Giant skeletons wave their arms in a procession, traditional and indigenous performers take to the stage, and people from all walks of life don skeleton face paint with bright florals. It's been a tradition in the city since 2010 and has been ranked among the top Day of the Dead festivals in the country by *USA Today*, Travel Channel, Lonely Planet, and others.

The event is spread throughout downtown Fort Lauderdale and broken up into three unique experiences, with a festival, stroll, and block party. On the folklorico stage, more than 100 performers bring traditional Mexican, Latin American, and indigenous music and dancing to the event. One of the biggest highlights of the day is the skeleton processional, with pros from the Puppet Network and the Puppet Guild of South Florida presenting giant skeletons as tall as 18 feet as they make their way through the Riverwalk

FORT LAUDERDALE DAY OF THE DEAD

WHAT: A Mexican tradition to honor the dead

WHERE: Throughout Fort Lauderdale

COST: Free to enter

PRO TIP: Not ready for the fun to end? There are after-parties until 2 a.m.

Jim Hammond, the event's founder, has decades of experience with puppetry, including a stint with Broadway's *The Lion King*.

Above: *Sugar skull face paint is a must for the Day of the Dead festival. Courtesy Felix Mizioznikov / Shutterstock.com*

Left: *The Skeleton Processional in downtown Fort Lauderdale. Courtesy tome213 / Shutterstock.com*

area. Finally, there is a block party along Himmarshee Street with more food trucks, DJs, music, indoor-outdoor bars, and dozens of vendors selling their unique creations.

The Day of the Dead festival hit hard times in 2023 when Fort Lauderdale was drenched in more than two feet of rain; countless families' homes were flooded, including puppetmaster and festival founder Jim Hammond's. However, he and the community rallied, and the show went on. Quite poetic, this story of resilience, for an event honoring the dead.

FLOAT LIKE A BUTTERFLY

Where is the butterfly capital of the world?

BUTTERFLY WORLD

WHAT: The attraction that put Coconut Creek on the map

WHERE: Tradewinds Park, 3600 W Sample Rd., Coconut Creek

COST: There is a fee for admission. Parking is free weekdays, but charged on weekends.

PRO TIP: Tradewinds Park is bisected by Sample Road; Butterfly World is on the south side of the park.

Monarch High School, Monarch Hill Renewable Energy Park, apartments named for butterflies—the butterfly theme in the Coconut Creek area is no coincidence. It is the Butterfly Capital of the World, after all.

Within Tradewinds Park in Coconut Creek is Butterfly World, a butterfly house with more than 20,000 butterflies and exotic birds spread over three acres of botanical gardens. Visitors enter and exit through vinyl strip doors, and staff use a duster to ensure that no butterflies make their great escape. Once inside the netted aviary, fluttering butterflies dance around waterfalls, tropical flowers, bridges, and a misting tunnel. Note that butterflies are attracted to bright colors; choose bright, colorful clothing for your trip to Butterfly World. Stand still for a bit, and a butterfly may land on you for the perfect photo op.

The park goes beyond the butterfly aviary, too. There's a lorikeet encounter, where guests can purchase a cup of nectar for $2 (cash only) to feed them; a

Above: *Children walk through the misting cave at the butterfly aviary. Photos courtesy Butterfly World*

Right: *A butterfly rests on a child's hand.*

Opposite: *A birdwing butterfly*

lake that can be crossed over via the Tinalandia Bridge, a replica of the one in Ecuador; an English rose garden; a garden gazebo; a laboratory; and an indoor bug zoo and butterfly museum. Hungry? Make a pit stop at the Mariposa Cafe.

When Butterfly World opened in 1988, it was the first butterfly house in the United States. An engineer by trade and a butterfly enthusiast by hobby, founder Ronald Boender was inspired by the now-closed London Butterfly House and built the gardens in Coconut Creek. Three decades later, Butterfly World is not just a huge draw for tourists, but also a working butterfly farm that is credited with helping save the Schaus Swallowtail.

Butterfly World offers discounts on tickets throughout the year, including Mother's Day, and is part of the South Florida Adventure Pass.

GIVE ME LIBERTY OR GIVE ME DEATH

What is the significance of the tree on the banks of the New River?

If you hear the sounds of rebellion in Huizenga Park, they're probably coming from the shade of the massive Bicentennial Liberty Tree.

It's a southern live oak that's made its home on the banks of the New River since 1976, the United States bicentennial. For the occasion, the city wanted to relocate a 200-year-old tree from the south side to the north side of the New River—a journey of less than a mile. Like many things, it was easier said than done. The tree turned out to be about 10 times heavier than anticipated, the Andrews Avenue bridge couldn't bear the load, and the city's 15-ton crane couldn't handle the job.

The city had to turn to a local company with a 300-ton crane and then send the tree up the river on a barge. The tree made it to its final destination successfully, but some shared their doubts with newspapers that it wouldn't survive because the move had been "bungled." Half a century later, it still provides plenty of shade to those who visit Huizenga Park.

The Liberty Tree is inspired by the original one in Boston, which was a popular gathering place for the Sons of Liberty to discuss their plans to rebel against the British. Over the years, other colonies followed suit with their own hidden-in-

---

Another notable tree that was moved within Fort Lauderdale is the century-old rain tree, which was relocated to make room for development. Its viability is still to be determined.

The Bicentennial Liberty Tree in Huizenga Park. Courtesy Fort Lauderdale Downtown Development Authority

plain-sight Liberty Trees, and 250 years later, Fort Lauderdale has its own symbol of freedom and patriotism.

After the terrorist attacks on Sept. 11, 2001, the city decided to rededicate the tree in honor of those who were killed, partnering with the Downtown Development Authority to do so on the one-year anniversary in 2002.

BICENTENNIAL LIBERTY TREE

WHAT: A live oak honoring America's independence and the victims of 9/11

WHERE: Huizenga Park, 32 E Las Olas Blvd., Fort Lauderdale

COST: Free to enter

PRO TIP: Another Liberty Tree in Greater Fort Lauderdale is in Plantation, at Rae Carole Armstrong Liberty Tree Park.

SANDY HOLIDAYS

How does Fort Lauderdale celebrate Christmas on the beach?

Fort Lauderdale tops out at a cool 76 degrees during December—not exactly the makings of a white Christmas. Not to worry, though, Olas the sandman comes around to get everyone into the spirit of things.

The 20-foot-tall sand "snowman" has been a Fort Lauderdale holiday tradition since 2015, when he made his first appearance on Fort Lauderdale Beach at A1A and Las Olas Boulevard (hence the name). Olas takes on a different look each year, from riding on a stand-up paddleboard to cruising on a Jet Ski, decked out in fishing gear, windsurfing, playing beach volleyball, preparing to hit the waves on his surfboard, or smiling at a selfie stick. No matter his get up, though, Olas is never without a hat and sunglasses. Sun safety is important this time of year, after all. What SPF do you think he prefers?

Olas makes his grand debut each year for the holiday season during Fort Lauderdale's Light Up the Beach celebration at Las Olas Oceanside Park, an evening of family fun with visits from Santa, music from local groups, a kids zone, and

OLAS THE SANDMAN

WHAT: A photo op for the ultimate Fort Lauderdale Christmas

WHERE: Las Olas Oceanside Park, 3000 E Las Olas Blvd., Fort Lauderdale

COST: Free to enter

PRO TIP: Olas is Spanish for "waves."

Olas the sandy snowman gets his name from nearby Las Olas Boulevard, which means "the waves" in Spanish.

Olas the Sandman comes out for the holiday season every year with a different outfit and activity. Courtesy City of Fort Lauderdale

plenty of photos. In fact, Olas makes plenty of rounds on social media. Passersby are encouraged to take a selfie with him with the hashtag #showusyourolas.

A ROCKIN' LIGHT SHOW

Is that a guitar-shaped hotel I see there?

Whether you're landing at Fort Lauderdale–Hollywood International Airport or driving on the Florida Turnpike, it's hard to miss the guitar-shaped hotel in Hollywood. By day, the sight of two guitars set back to back and six strings running up the sides of the 36-story hotel is impressive enough. At night, though, it really comes to life.

Each evening, the hotel at the Seminole Hard Rock Hotel & Casino Hollywood puts on a 10-minute light show after sunset with LED lights bursting with color to coincide with music. The colors of the hotel change, too, according to different holidays and happenings. Think pink for Breast Cancer Awareness, the American flag on the Fourth of July, and a countdown on New Year's Eve. When the Florida Panthers won the Stanley Cup in in 2024 and 2025, the hotel lit up in red with the words "Florida Panthers" and "Go Cats Go!" scrolling across. With lights shooting out of the top of the neck of the guitar, the lights project an impressive 20,000 feet into the air at night.

GUITAR HOTEL

WHAT: A rockin' hotel that lights up the night sky

WHERE: 4783–4787 Lucky St., Hollywood

COST: Free to enter

PRO TIP: Keep in mind that the light show might vary slightly, especially during the time change in the spring and fall.

Music fans will enjoy the casino, which has authentic outfits on displays from A-list stars like Madonna and Taylor Swift to Cher and Johnny Cash.

Above: *Seminole Hard Rock Hotel and Casino. Photos courtesy Seminole Hard Rock Hotel and Casino*

Left: *The lights project 20,000 feet into the air from the neck of the guitar.*

The Guitar Hotel was part of a massive $1.5 billion expansion that began in October 2019, with 638 hotel guest rooms and a 34-story Oasis Tower. Other attractions of note at the hotel and casino: 16 restaurants, four bars, six swimming pools, the Hard Rock live entertainment space, the nightclub and day-club DAER, a 42,000-square-foot spa, and enough shopping to double as a mall.

DINNER AND A SHOW

What's the deal with the red-and-white riverboats?

There's plenty of boat-watching to be had on Fort Lauderdale's canals, its rivers, and the Intracoastal, and one standout is the *Jungle Queen* riverboat—a source of both entertainment and education. Guests hop aboard the boat to see the luxe mansions on Millionaire's Row, learn the history of Fort Lauderdale, and enjoy dinner and a Polynesian-themed show.

The original boat was built in Jacksonville and brought down to Fort Lauderdale by Captain Al Starts in 1935, launching a beloved tradition. The first *Jungle Queen* was 60 feet long and could accommodate 50 passengers. He also built the Jungle Queen Village, featuring a Seminole trading post, alligator wrestling, and Seminole arts and crafts. Today, the company is owned by the third generation of the Faber family and has expanded to four riverboats—named simply *Jungle Queen 1, 2, 3,* and *4*—offering 90-minute sightseeing cruises twice daily and an Island Dinner & Show cruise in the evening. During the dinner show, guests are whisked away to Jungle Queen Island for an all-

JUNGLE QUEEN

WHAT: Enjoy dinner and a show aboard a historic riverboat.

WHERE: Embark from Bahia Mar Yachting Center, 801 Seabreeze Blvd., Fort Lauderdale

COST: Prices vary, please see their website for details.

PRO TIP: The Jungle Queen is cashless; make sure you bring a credit or debit card.

Tiki culture is big in Fort Lauderdale's history, from shows on the Jungle Queen to the Mai Kai Restaurant, which underwent a major renovation.

Above: *Passengers on the* Jungle Queen *can learn about local history and get a look at the multi-million dollar homes on the river.*

Left: *There are four riverboats in the* Jungle Queen *fleet. Photos courtesy* Jungle Queen

you-can-eat barbecue feast and a show with Polynesian hula and fire dancers, fire eaters, drummers, and other island entertainment.

As if the Jungle Queen enterprise weren't enough, Starts also had big plans for what he called "Spaceland Aluminum City," which varied from an entertainment district on the beach to a contained theme park. Those never came to fruition, but his legacy endures with the Jungle Queen riverboats still traversing Fort Lauderdale's waterways to this day.

ANIMAL KINGDOM

What's that big blue bunny on Wilton Drive?

Thirteen feet tall, 6,500 pieces of hand-cut mirrored glass, six months of artistic labor—this is all the more impressive since it's on a blue bunny sculpture.

Thunderbunny by Hunt Slonem has become a fixture on Wilton Drive in Wilton Manors, which is saying a lot considering all the public art that stitches the city together. The bunny arrived in the Island City thanks to a loan from the New River Art Gallery in Fort Lauderdale, but it was so well received that the artist agreed to make it a permanent part of the Drive. "I'm for art being in public places where it's seen," he said. "It shouldn't be in just art fairs or private collections."

Slonem, who was born in the year of the rabbit, is known for his rabbit artwork, particularly on canvas, as well as butterflies and birds. When he created *Thunderbunny* in 2021, it was the first time in two decades that he had played with mosaic work. According to the artist, the piece is worth about $300,000.

THUNDERBUNNY

WHAT: A bright blue mosaic bunny on Wilton Drive

WHERE: Justin Flippen Park, 2109 Wilton Dr., Wilton Manors

COST: Free to enter

PRO TIP: To explore public art in Wilton Manors, Pick up a copy of the In Sight map at various locations around town as well as online at wiltonmanors.gov

New River Fine Art, which helped secure the sculpture, is located on the Las Olas Boulevard shopping thoroughfare and carries pieces by Henri Matisse, Keith Haring, Andy Warhol, Pablo Picasso, Salvador Dali, and more.

Thunderbunny by Hunt Slonem

Wilton Manors has more than two dozen sculptures throughout the city as well as a number of murals. On the Sculpture Walk, art lovers can find giant candy hearts, a melting popsicle, juicy slices of orange, a colorful manatee, and more. As for murals, one of the most defining in the city is the "Love Wins" rainbow bridge that connects Wilton Manors to Fort Lauderdale.

UNDER THE SEA

Where can you meet a mermaid?

If Ariel were to pick a beach to wash up on, it would probably be Fort Lauderdale Beach. There are mermaids just steps (er, strokes) away at the B Ocean Resort, after all.

The hotel's iconic Wreck Bar is designed like the inside of a pirate ship, with a wall of portholes that guests can use to see the peekaboo swimming pool for aquatic shows. Multiple times a week the bar hosts mermaid shows, with ladies in fish tails swimming past the windows, blowing bubble kisses, and performing underwater tricks. Brunch Under the Sea is a family-friendly show with mermaids swimming past the restaurant, and guests also have the chance to attend a meet-and-greet with the mermaids topside at the pool. For the adults, the Siren Serenade show on Saturday nights is a 21-and-older experience that's a unique night out on the town while sipping on cocktails like the Sunken Treasure, Stormy Seas, or Make Me a Mermaid.

MERMAID SHOW AT THE WRECK BAR

WHAT: Enjoy a drink while gazing at mermaids through a porthole.

WHERE: B Ocean Resort, 1140 Seabreeze Blvd., Fort Lauderdale

COST: Admission varies by event.

PRO TIP: Dining With Mermaids on Thursdays and Fridays allows you to enjoy the mermaids without an additional cost.

The Wreck Bar was one of the backdrops of the film *Analyze This* with Robert De Niro and Billy Crystal.

Mermaids have been swimming past the portholes of the Wreck Bar since the '50s. Courtesy B Ocean Resort Fort Lauderdale Beach

The B Ocean Resort was built in 1956 and was originally known as the Yankee Clipper, designed in the shape of a ship; a night here would run you $8. Fort Lauderdale was considered a quiet getaway from the hubbub of Miami, and celebrities like Marilyn Monroe and Joe DiMaggio (the Yankees had spring training in Fort Lauderdale at the time) would head to the Wreck Bar for mermaid shows and the Polynesian Room on the second floor to indulge in the en vogue tiki culture.

A STUDENT OF HISTORY

Where was the first school for black children in Broward County?

The history of black Broward has its tragedies and its triumphs, and this story is told within the walls of the Old Dillard Museum.

The classrooms of this school, which was originally built for black children, have been converted to exhibit spaces, including the Dillard Sports Zone showcasing athletes and coaches who graduated from the school; the Sankofa Room filled with West African items and oral histories from elders; the Jazz Lounge celebrating musicians and performers who are Dillard alumni; and the Heritage Room with its replica classroom and Tree of Knowledge, each of its leaves dedicated to a black pioneer in Broward County. Though understated, one of the most moving spaces is the My Soul is a Witness room—named for the book by Deborah Work—with walls filled with photos of sharecroppers, the tragic lynching of Rubin Stacy, and segregation; also presented are the stories of major pioneers in education, business, faith, and medicine, such as Sylvia Aldridge, Dr. James Sistrunk, Dr. Niara Sudarkasa, and George Burrows. In addition, the exhibit presents the light-hearted side of growing up on Sistrunk Boulevard and the royal prom courts. On permanent display is a school desk sitting in soil and covered in books, pennies, dirt, and produce, a statement on the dichotomy of a student balancing sharecropping with their studies.

The Dillard School was built on land purchased for just $1 from the city's founders, Frank and Ivy Stranahan, thanks

---

Celebrated jazz musician Cannonball Adderley was hired to teach music at Dillard High School in 1948.

Above: *A replica classroom at the Old Dillard Museum; the mismatched desks are indicative of students receiving hand-me-downs from white students.*

Left: *Old Dillard Museum was the first school in Broward County for black children.*

to a suggestion from their housekeeper, Annie T. Reed. As the city grew, more schools were built, but the original has kept its place in the city's history. Today, the Old Dillard Museum is listed on the National Register of Historic Sites, and Dillard High School is just two miles away. It's a part of a legacy of greatness rising above inequity and injustice.

OLD DILLARD MUSEUM

WHAT: A celebration of black excellence in Broward County

WHERE: 1009 NW Fourth St., Fort Lauderdale

COST: Free to enter; donations welcomed

PRO TIP: The museum is next door to the current Walker Elementary School; Dillard once was called Walker before it became a high school.

LIKE MOTHER, LIKE DAUGHTER

MY MAMA'S BOOKS, RECORDS AND CAFE

WHAT: A shop for records, books, food, and community

WHERE: 218 E Dania Beach Blvd., Dania Beach

COST: Free to enter

PRO TIP: The store does have a small, free parking lot.

Is there a place for music, reading, and community?

At My Mama's in Dania Beach, a sweet black-and-white photo says it all, an image of three generations of women. "We are all mamas," says owner Julia Harrison.

She was inspired by her mother, Susan, who was a part of a free-thinking, progressive collective in the 1950s, and her father, a poet and activist. At My Mama's, Harrison brings together music, literature, and food to create a space that fosters creativity and friendship. Guests walking into this Dania Beach store are welcomed by walls lined with both new and used books—from graphic novels to memoirs and children's books—and pages filled with all things Florida. Then there are the racks of records spanning all genres—country, opera, jazz, punk, alternative, soundtracks, Latin, and more.

Some come to read, others to find more vinyl to add to their collections. Either way, there's a menu of smoothies, coffees, teas, and sweet, and savory foods to

Records of all genres at My Mama's

enjoy. Pull up a chair at the mismatched table sets throughout My Mama's, the result of a lifetime of collecting eclectic furniture, each decorated with a vase filled with fresh flowers.

Throughout the week, the store hosts Open Mic Tuesdays, story time and family music on Saturdays, and pop-up events like paint-and-sip gatherings and game nights. In the works are local author readings, upcycling workshops, clothing swaps, and other events to bring people together.

Definitely approved by Mama.

My Mama's also has a selection of signed books for sale, as well as rare and hard-to-find selections of books and music.

NO LIMIT

Where can artists play with light, sound, and visuals?

Creating software to capture the energy exploding from a drum . . . Spanish protest poetry married with coding . . . an LED forest wall—the exhibits at MAD Arts Museum are no ordinary collection.

A fine art photographer who runs a local marketing firm, founder Marc Aptakin started a version of the museum in 2016, renting out a warehouse that was open for artists to experiment. With its success, his company purchased a building in 2020 and has turned it into an artists' playground that can be experienced by the public. At 50,000 square feet, MAD Arts Museum is filled with exhibits incorporating sound, light projection, animation, robotics, coding, and other tech elements into art for a multidisciplinary experience.

The museum's reach has extended past its walls, too, as it is part of the growing art festival IGNITE, which takes place throughout Fort Lauderdale and Hollywood. MAD Arts has worked with artists to incorporate light and sound into their public displays, such as projecting film onto sculptures; it's

MAD ARTS MUSEUM

WHAT: An experimental museum for artists with out-of-the-box ideas

WHERE: 481 S Federal Hwy., Dania Beach

COST: There is a fee for entry.

PRO TIP: Photos at the museum are allowed and welcomed.

The space that houses the MAD Arts Museum used to be the Museum of Amazing Things; a fitting successor for the building.

Above: *"Quantum Jungle" by Robin Baumgarten*

Left: *"Luminescent Sylva" by MadLabs*

what artists refer to as "phygital"—a mix of the physical and digital worlds.

The possibilities are endless in this marriage of art and technology, lending to a rotation of temporary exhibits while also being grounded in seven pieces in the permanent collection. MAD Arts hosts artist workshops and reaches out to underprivileged youth to show them the career possibilities in tech.

BATHING BEAUTIES

How does a beauty pageant sell houses?

Enveloped between Davie Boulevard and Marina Mile, Croissant Park is a buzzing neighborhood with parks, schools, a swimming pool, and an active civic association. A century ago it was untarnished land promoted by ladies in bathing suits.

With Fort Lauderdale on the rise, real estate developer G. Frank Croissant stepped onto the scene with the mission to sell the Croissant Park neighborhood. He touted himself as the "World's Greatest Salesman." In 1924, the Placidena Field Office was built, a Mediterranean Revival building that served as the sales office with 146 employees pitching Croissant Park. Prospective homebuyers were treated to an alfresco pitch from a gazebo, where they could pick a lot for their future home. It was advertised as "the garden spot of tropical Florida."

Croissant came up with creative marketing tactics to promote Croissant Park, including fish fries, concerts, a song competition, and a trip to Costa Rica for top salespeople. The most unique, though, that is still talked about to this day, is the Miss Lauderdale Bathing Beauty contest of 1925, open to single women ages 18 to 25. A newspaper published a photo of each woman in their bathing suit, and readers were encouraged to vote for their favorite. Eleanor Adams won, crowning her Miss Lauderdale of Croissant Park with 107,300 votes out of the 700,000 cast. She also won a 10-day trip to the National Bathing Beauty Revue in Atlantic City.

After the land boom of the 1920s, the Croissant Park Administration Building was neglected for decades. In 1998, it was purchased for $300,000, restored, and was added to the

---

The population of Fort Lauderdale in 1920 was only about 5,600 people, showing the popularity of the contest.

Fifteen local women vied for the title of Miss Lauderdale, a part of a marketing campaign to promote Croissant Park. Courtesy History Fort Lauderdale

National Register of Historic Places in 2001. Today, the building is used for office and retail space.

CROISSANT PARK

WHAT: An unassuming office building with a history of pageantry

WHERE: 1421 S Andrews Ave., Fort Lauderdale

COST: Free to enter

PRO TIP: Before it was named after G. Frank Croissant, it was called Palm City and then Placidena.

LIGHTS, CAMERA, ACTION

Does Fort Lauderdale remind you of the South Sea?

Greater Fort Lauderdale has served as the backdrop for plenty of Hollywood movies—*Caddyshack*, *Happy Gilmore*, *Where the Boys Are*, *Analyze This*, *Donnie Brasco*, *Midnight Cowboy*, and *Rock of Ages*, to name a few. The very first, though, was all the way back in 1919.

NEW RIVER

WHAT: The setting for a Hollywood silent film

WHERE: New River in Fort Lauderdale

COST: Free to enter

PRO TIP: You can watch *The Idol Dancer* on YouTube.

Director D. W. Griffith—who filmed *Birth of a Nation*—and cameraman G. W. "Billy" Bitzer came to Fort Lauderdale with a crew of 50 people to film *The Idol Dancer*. To them, the town's New River was the perfect backdrop for the romance set in the South Seas. But before they could start they needed lodging, so they convinced the not-yet-opened Hotel Broward to open its doors in exchange for the crew helping complete the hotel—including painting walls and putting up curtains.

Ready to film, Griffith hired local fishermen to boat the cast members to their shoots, schoolgirls to work as extras in a wedding scene, and Seminole people to play the role of island natives. The starring roles went to actors Richard Barthelmess and Clarine Seymour; it would be Seymour's last movie, as she died of pneumonia a month after the premiere.

In the movie, Seymour plays Mary, a French-Javanese dancer who is torn between two lovers; their love is tested when the island is attacked. Barthelmess's character, a drunk, wins Mary's love when he sees the error of his ways. When *The Idol Dancer* was released, it was advertised as a "tale of

Director D. W. Griffith filming on the banks of the New River. Courtesy State Archives of Florida

true love and wild adventure among the cannibals, headhunters, and black birders of the South Sea Isles."

Griffith reportedly said of Fort Lauderdale, "There may be a more beautiful river in the world than the New River, which flows through the heart of your city, but if so I have never seen it."

The Hotel Broward did not stand the test of time; more tourists were interested in staying closer to the beach and the building was demolished in 1974.

WELCOME, MR. PRESIDENT

How did Fort Lauderdale residents greet President Harding?

When Warren G. Harding was elected president in 1920, he had plans to go on tour to greet his constituents. That included a two-week trip through Florida, from St. Augustine all the way south to Miami.

NEW RIVER

WHAT: Kidnapping President-Elect Warren G. Harding

WHERE: New River in Fort Lauderdale

COST: Free to enter

PRO TIP: Legend has it that the golf club he used is at History Fort Lauderdale; unfortunately, staff say it's just a golf club from the era, not actually used by Harding.

But not Fort Lauderdale.

Residents were disappointed when they discovered his itinerary; they had planned for the president-elect to make a pitstop in the riverfront town, going so far as to outfit the yacht Granada III with a banner reading "Welcome Harding." Apparently the White House only thought it was necessary for Harding to wave from the houseboat *Victoria* as he made his way from his stop in Palm Beach.

Fort Lauderdale wouldn't have any of it though—they had prepared for his visit, and he was going to stop whether he liked it or not. As the houseboat floated through the New River, residents managed to grab ahold of it and forced it to

---

President Warren Harding did not complete his presidency; he died in 1923 and was succeeded by his vice president, Calvin Coolidge.

Top: *President Warren G. Harding spends time golfing with residents after being "kidnapped" from his house boat while touring Florida. Photos courtesy History Fort Lauderdale*

Bottom Left: *President Warren G. Harding waves from his friend's houseboat while passing through Fort Lauderdale.*

Bottom Right: *Fort Lauderdale residents were prepared to welcome President Warren G. Harding to their town.*

dock, essentially kidnapping the most powerful man in the nation. Harding appears to have been a good sport, though, and security was not what it is today. He wound up spending a few hours fishing and playing golf—as you do during a trip to Florida.

JUST BREATHE

What is that sculpture of a woman ripping open her ribcage?

There are plenty of Instagrammable moments around Fort Lauderdale, and one that's in many a visitor's feed is *Thrive* in front of the Flow apartments.

Located in downtown Fort Lauderdale, the 27-foot-tall sculpture by Daniel Popper is of a woman pulling at her ribcage, revealing a lush, fern-covered interior. It sounds graphic, but the woman's face is at ease, as if she's at peace revealing her heart. The sculpture is especially moving at night, with the uplights adding power to the piece.

Popper is an artist hailing from Cape Town, South Africa, and his works around the world follow a similar look of incorporating nature into the bodies of women. Some are made from concrete, others appear to be created out of a tree's root system. But their eyes are closed, perhaps in a permanent state of meditation. For *Thrive*, Popper used glass fiber reinforced concrete, steel, and fiberglass. He explained that even with the meticulousness

THRIVE

WHAT: A larger-than-life sculpture by a South African artist

WHERE: Flow, 301 SW First Ave., Fort Lauderdale

COST: Free to enter

PRO TIP: Want more art? The NSU Museum of Art Fort Lauderdale is less than a five-minute walk away.

Another one of Daniel Popper's sculptures, *Lumen*, can be found in Miami's Wynwood art district, about an hour south of Fort Lauderdale.

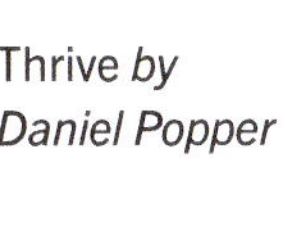

Thrive *by Daniel Popper*

of urban planning, nature always finds a way to creep through the cracks.

Thrive was inspired by a similar wooden sculpture he completed in Mexico, *Ven a la Luz*, and Flow (formerly Society Las Olas) commissioned the artist to create one for the entry to the apartment complex. Installed in pieces in 2020, it's hard to miss while walking through downtown to the Riverwalk.

GOVERNOR BROWARD

Where did Broward County get its name?

Broward County's name *almost* comes from that of a French general—Napoleon Bonaparte Broward.

He was born in Duval County in north Florida in 1857. He became an orphan at age 12, but despite this rough start in life, he was elected sheriff of Duval in 1889 and would go on to serve in the Florida House of Representatives and be elected governor in 1904. Some of his accomplishments include promoting the formation of a state university system, toughening child labor laws, and—unfortunately—leading the campaign to drain the Everglades, which at the time were seen as a "pestilence-ridden swamp" that could be turned into useful farmland. Broward died in 1910, and in 1915 Broward County was founded and named in his honor; the original name being considered was Everglades County.

NAPOLEON BONAPARTE BROWARD

WHAT: The county's namesake and a controversial statue

WHERE: Broward County Courthouse, 201 SE Sixth St., Fort Lauderdale

COST: Free to enter

PRO TIP: The courthouse is connected to the Broward County Main Jail in the middle of prime real estate downtown.

Also in his honor, a statue of Broward was erected in the lobby of the Broward County Courthouse in Fort Lauderdale in 1993. However, it was revealed that the former governor was openly racist and separatist, encouraging Congress "to purchase territory, either domestic or foreign, and provide means to purchase the property of the negroes at a reasonable price and to transport them to the territory purchased by the United States." He added, "The white people have no time to make excuses for the shortcomings of the negro."

Governor Napoleon Bonaparte Broward. Courtesy University of Florida Digital Collection

The TJ Reddick Bar Association, a group of black lawyers, led the charge to have the statue removed from the courthouse. In 2017, the statue was removed in the middle of the night and reportedly put into storage, possibly to be put on display in a museum at a later date.

No counties in Florida ended up being named Everglades County; there is an Everglades City, though, in Collier County.

IT'S A JUNGLE OUT THERE

Has there ever been a zoo in Fort Lauderdale?

In 1936, the McKillop-Hutton Lion Farm opened in a former rock quarry and served as a breeding farm for zoos and circuses around the country. Local kids could come by to watch the lions, tigers, and leopards being trained. Three years later, animal trainer Clyde Beatty purchased the lion farm and turned it into a tourist attraction. It was also the ideal winter home for him and his wife, aerialist Harriett Evans.

Beatty was known nationwide for his death-defying tricks, like entering an arena with lions, tigers, cougars, and hyenas, sometimes all at the same time. Often he carried a whip and had a revolver at his side, and he was able to get a Bengal tiger to roll over. Locals could hear lions and tigers at all hours of the day, and it wasn't unusual for a monkey to escape over the walls of the zoo.

MCKILLOP-HUTTON LION FARM AND CLYDE BEATTY ZOO

WHAT: A short-lived zoo and lion farm in Fort Lauderdale

WHERE: Gateway Shopping Center, 1900 E Sunrise Blvd., Fort Lauderdale

COST: Free

PRO TIP: To see animals, check out Flamingo Gardens in Davie, a sanctuary for American crocodiles, birds of prey, a black bear, river otters, and other animals.

However, Fort Lauderdale was growing, and not everyone was thrilled with the idea of living next door to a zoo. In addition, zoning regulations were getting stricter; Beatty was

---

Lions can be viewed at Lion Country Safari in Loxahatchee, about an hour north of Fort Lauderdale.

Clyde Beatty. Courtesy State Archive of Florida

forced to sell the zoo, and he and his circus went back on the road. Even with the town leaving a bad taste in their mouth, Harriett was buried in Fort Lauderdale when she died.

Today, the area where the zoo and lion farm were located is a shopping center, home to the iconic Gateway movie theatre as well as shops and restaurants.

SEE YOU LATER, ALLIGATOR

Why is the alligator at Flamingo Gardens named Elvis?

Why have a pet monkey when you can have a pet alligator? That seemed to be the logic when crafting the character of Sonny Crockett on *Miami Vice*.

That alligator's name was Elvis, and his character was the former mascot for the University of Florida. In reality, Elvis was a 8.5-foot, 300-pound American alligator who lived at Gator World in Davie. His owner, George Harwell, would shuttle him to *Miami Vice* shoots along with Elvis's stunt double, a smaller alligator named Presley, who would step in when Elvis needed a break. During this time, visitors to the zoo could see Elvis in his enclosure with a sign announcing that he was *the* Elvis from *Miami Vice*. One time, Elvis managed to escape from his chain leash and remove the tape around his mouth, and he took a swim in Biscayne Bay—a story that made the paper. "Alligators tire very easily . . . that scene was kind of strenuous," Harwell told the *Miami Herald* in October 1984 about Elvis's escape after being asked to walk 15 feet.

While Gator World is no longer at Flamingo Gardens (it closed in 1990), Elvis's memory lives on. Elvis the Third resides at the sanctuary with his partner, Priscilla. The pair was rescued from the illegal pet trade, and in 2025 the two celebrated their anniversary with a party.

FLAMINGO GARDENS

WHAT: Home to an alligator acting sensation

WHERE: 3750 S Flamingo Rd., Davie

COST: There is a fee to visit. Discounts are available for seniors and children.

PRO TIP: While you're there, don't forget to see Josh the black bear, river otters, roaming peacocks, and rescued big cats.

Elvis III rests in his pool at Flamingo Gardens.

See even more alligators in nearby Sawgrass Recreation Park in the middle of the Everglades National Park, home to more than 200,000 alligators.

HOLLY JOLLY AHOY

What's a Fort Lauderdale tradition viewed by millions?

A Fort Lauderdale tradition since 1971, the Winterfest Boat Parade was originally hosted by a few guys drinking beers on the river and has grown into the self-proclaimed "Biggest Show on H20."

The 12-mile route takes a parade of boats—lit up to suit the year's theme—from the Stranahan House up the Intracoastal to Pompano Beach, and back down to the Broward Center. Locals purchase tickets for a spot at one of the VIP viewing areas, gather at homes located on the New River and Intracoastal for watch parties, or throw out a picnic blanket to watch the boats go by. There's a contest, too, with judges and the public making their choices in categories by boat size and type, with prizes for the top vote-getters in theme, lights, entertainment, and overall.

WINTERFEST BOAT PARADE

WHAT: A 12-mile boat parade for the holidays

WHERE: New River and Intracoastal

COST: Free to enter

PRO TIP: The parade route fills up quickly; make plans ahead of time for parking or make a reservation at a local restaurant to watch the show.

Of course, in Fort Lauderdale, there are parties to lead up to the party. In anticipation of the Winterfest Boat Parade, there are events such as the elaborate Black Tie Ball at the Seminole Hard Rock Hotel & Casino, family fun day, and the event poster debut; each year, an artist is tasked with creating the official event poster based on the year's theme. There's also the announcement of the celebrity grand marshal for the parade. Past grand marshals include Boyz II Men, Kim Kardashian, Mario Lopez, Joan Rivers, Dan Marino, Regis Philbin, Pitbull, and Flo Rida. The very first grand marshal in 1983 was NBC meteorologist Willard

Boats big and small are decked out in lights and holiday decor for the Winterfest Boat Parade. Courtesy Albert Barr / Shutterstock.com

Scott. In 1986, Bob Hope filmed his Christmas special with the Winterfest Boat Parade as a backdrop.

While the event takes place in Fort Lauderdale, it reaches millions: the event is televised up the eastern seaboard. Lucky us, though, we've got a front-row seat.

The Winterfest Foundation hosts local kids at the boat parade, an annual art contest for local elementary school students, and a Water Safety Day.

FOR WHOM THE BELL TOLLS

What's the deal with the giant bell at the Stranahan House?

A trip to the Stranahan House is a rite of passage for Broward County youngsters. With docents leading the way, countless kids have gone through the house of Ivy and Frank Stranahan, considered the founders of Fort Lauderdale. One of the highlights is lining up with classmates to ring the giant ferry bell toward the back of the house, facing the New River.

Ivy rented out four rooms in the house to E. J. and Shirley Blackwell, who opened the Pioneer House Restaurant in 1940. Eventually it grew to hundreds of seats on the patio spread all the way to the seawall, and Ivy never raised the monthly rent for them. At the restaurant, kids could ring the ferry bell when boats passed by—especially the *Jungle Queen*, as the captain would honk the horn in reply. However, sometime in the 1960s the bell was moved farther away from the riverfront and ended up in the parking lot, then finally in the backyard of Elsie Blackwell, E. J.'s mother. It seemed to disappear forever after that.

The ferry bell

The bell's whereabouts were unknown until the late 1980s, when the house had been converted into a museum and property caretaker John Della-Cerra (who still works at the museum!) was picking up ceramics donations from Nan Knox, the founder of the local Boys and Girls Club. In her backyard, he noticed an overturned

Caretaker John Della-Cerra rings the bell at the Stranahan House.

HISTORIC STRANAHAN HOUSE MUSEUM

WHAT: Home of Fort Lauderdale's founders and a bell that went missing in action for decades

WHERE: 335 SE 6th Ave., Fort Lauderdale

COST: Tickets are available for purchase. There are discounts available for seniors, students, and children.

PRO TIP: The bell is steps away from the replica trading post, which is what the house started as when Frank Stranahan doubled as the area's first postmaster.

bell. Was this the Stranahan House bell? Probably, Knox said—this house used to belong to the Blackwells. With the help of a local funeral home truck and some strong hands, a group managed to pick up the pieces of the bell and bring it back to the Stranahan House, where it was restored and re-installed.

Now it's back where it belongs, at the Stranahan House, waiting for kids to ring it.

Inside the Stranahan House is a safe built into the stairwell; it's jokingly called Fort Lauderdale's first bank since Frank Stranahan stored people's money there. Fun fact, it never locked.

SEE YOUR GYPSY

Who was the first woman to get a concealed-carry license in Broward?

Gypsy Graves's resume reads like an adventure novel—the founder of a natural history museum, a member of the Explorer's Club, the first licensed female horse trainer in Kentucky, and the first woman in Broward County to get a concealed-carry license.

Graves made an indelible mark on Fort Lauderdale by unearthing thousands of years of South Florida history with the Broward County Archaeological Society. She took part in the discovery of prehistoric tools, spears, and bones, all showing that man was in the area as far back as 3,000 BCE. In 1990, she led an all-woman archaeological team—All Women's Archaeological Research Expedition, a first—in Egypt, to search for the statue of Pharaoh Amenhotep III in Thebes. The trip was chronicled in a CBS documentary, *Women of Intrigue*.

She founded the Graves Museum of Archaeology and Natural History in Fort Lauderdale; it moved to Dania Beach

RIO VISTA

WHAT: The neighborhood where Gypsy Graves's 1926 house was located

WHERE: Southeast of the New River and Federal Highway

COST: Free to enter

PRO TIP: While Gypsy Graves's natural history museum is no more, there is the Palm Beach County Museum of Natural History in Wellington, about an hour north of Fort Lauderdale.

"Gypsy" was a nickname for Gypsophila, the scientific name for baby's breath flowers; the name was bestowed upon her by her father and it stuck for the rest of her life.

Photo courtesy of Sun Sentential

in 1993. The museum housed dinosaur bones and archaeological finds. Naturalist Marjory Stoneman Douglas was a guest speaker. Unfortunately, the museum closed in 2004, in debt and with a feuding board.

Graves lived in a historic home in the Rio Vista neighborhood; according to local legend its previous owners had mob ties, and the St. Valentine's Day Massacre of 1929 in Chicago was planned there. The home was razed in 2005, to the disappointment of locals; many called it "The Gypsy Graves House."

Graves died in 2021 when she was 91—and yes, her concealed-carry license was mentioned in the obituary.

BURGER JOINT

Where can you get a classic burger?

A Fort Lauderdale hamburger institution has a golden arch over the roof . . . no, not those golden arches.

Jack's Old Fashioned Hamburgers has been a part of the casual and always reliable dining scene since 1971, when Jack Berry opened the restaurant on Federal Highway in Fort Lauderdale. The menu has remained small and simple over the decades: burgers, sandwiches, hot dogs, sodas, thick milkshakes, and root beer floats. All fresh and never frozen, of course, and the restaurant opens at 10:30 a.m. for those early burger cravings.

JACK'S HAMBURGERS

WHAT: A classic burger joint

WHERE: 4201 N Federal Hwy., Oakland Park

COST: Free to enter

PRO TIP: Get the reusable cup to get $1 refills on your next visit.

In 1972, Berry opened a second hamburger joint, this time in Pompano Beach on Cypress Road. Both locations are still open and have kept their old-school charm. The walls are paneled with wood, a jukebox plays oldies and classic rock, and the table numbers that guests are given have celebrities from yesteryear on them, from Elvis and the Beatles to James Dean.

Berry found a home in Fort Lauderdale after bouncing around the country working in restaurants, in sales, and at odd jobs. This included hitchhiking from St. Louis to Los Angeles when he was 15 years old. He moved to Fort Lauderdale in 1959, working as a maitre d' at a friend's Italian restaurant.

Having a burger at Jack's is like grilling at a friend's house; the meat for the burgers is ground fresh daily and each burger is made to order.

Left: *The jukebox plays golden oldies and classic rock.*

Below: *The wood-paneled dining room with stained glass light fixtures evokes classic dining.*

Then he took a chance on his own dream and opened Jack's Old Fashioned Hamburgers. When Berry died in 2011, a memorial was hosted at Hugh's Culinary, and everyone in town was invited.

Out front is a banner reading "50 years, and still flipping!" Here's to another 50 years of juicy burgers.

POP CULTURE FANDOM

Where can you buy comic books?

Whether you're team Marvel or team DC, you're welcome at Tate's Comics + Toys + More, an area institution for all things pop culture.

Located in an unassuming strip mall in Lauderhill, the store is a sprawling 10,000 square feet of comic books and graphic novels, toys, artwork, children's books, Japanese snacks, art supplies, and gifts. Visitors can spend hours making their way through the labyrinth, poring over comic books straight off the press as well as vintage classics safely stored behind glass cases. It's here that parents introduce their children to the world of superheroes, especially with a life-size Spiderman shooting webs by a bookshelf, R2-D2 standing guard by a display of Star Wars action figures and ephemera, and a recreation of Han Solo trapped in carbonite. Tate's transports you to the days of Spawn, Alf, Archie, the Transformers, a slew of shows from the '80s and '90s, as well as Japanese imports like Akira.

TATE'S COMICS + TOYS + MORE

WHAT: Heaven for comic book and pop culture fans

WHERE: 4566 N University Dr., Lauderhill

COST: Free to enter

PRO TIP: Customers cannot carry large bags around the store; you can check your bag at the front and retrieve it on your way out.

Tate's is named for its founder, Tate Ottati, who opened the store when he was just a senior in high school in 1993. The store has exploded in size since then, and in 2007 Ottati and

---

Check out Tate's website for its calendar of events, including its anniversary sales, meet and greets, and comic book signings.

Above: *Tate's also has new comics, right off the presses.*

Right: *A life-sized Spiderman next to action figures and books*

his wife, Amanda, opened Bear and Bird Boutique + Gallery in the store's loft, a gallery of art prints, greeting cards, jewelry, cooking supplies, patches, and other gifts. From here, looking down at the first floor, you really get an understanding of how expansive Tate's is, and why it's been the go-to for decades.

SEMINOLE GIRL

Who is the little girl walking along the New River with a crane and an alligator?

Made of bronze, a little 5-year-old Seminole girl stands mid-stride along the banks of the New River, a smile on her face as she's accompanied by her friends, a baby alligator and a crane. In her hands is a fan of palmetto leaves.

It's *Florida: A Seminole Girl* by Nilda Comas, an 8-foot-tall sculpture that was installed at Stranahan's Landing. She was inspired by Florida's 500th anniversary in 2013 and a visit to Ah-Tah-Thi-Ki, the Seminole Tribe's museum for history and culture, where she met with community leaders. With their support, the sculpture was unveiled in 2015, just across the river from the Stranahan House. This is significant, as Ivy Stranahan was an advocate for the Seminole Tribe, opening her classrooms

FLORIDA: SEMINOLE GIRL

WHAT: A bronze sculpture honoring the Seminole Tribe of Florida and the state's 500th year

WHERE: Smoker Family Park, 501 S New River Dr. E, Fort Lauderdale

COST: Free to enter

PRO TIP: When you use your phone to take a picture, you'll notice that a website will pop up, as if you had scanned a QR code. Click on it and you'll hear a recording of Everglades and Seminole children singing.

The Ahfachkee School—Eláponke for "happy"—is a kindergarten through 12th grade school that emphasizes learning about Seminole culture and the Eláponke language.

Seminole Girl *by Nilda Comas*

to the tribe's children and even lobbying the US government to maintain the tribe's benefits.

Hundreds of tiles cover the pedestal of the statue, honoring donors who helped fund the piece. On the base are colorful tiles that were painted by children from the Ahfachkee School on the Big Cypress Reservation.

Comas's work can be found in other places in Fort Lauderdale. She sculpted *The Li'l Blader* at Colee Hammock Park, *Play Ball* at Holiday Park, *Tequesta* at Lewis Landing Park, and a bust of Robert Elmore at Broward College's library.

TURTLE POWER

Where can you watch baby sea turtles waddle to the ocean?

Ever wondered why the lights by the beach are an amber color part of the year? It's because it's sea turtle season, and hatchlings need to be able to follow the moon back into the ocean and not be distracted by man-made lights.

Running from March to October, sea turtle season is a big deal in Greater Fort Lauderdale, with conservation groups roping off found nests on the beaches to make sure that visitors don't step over them.

Five sea turtle species make their way to the area annually to lay their eggs, with the top three being loggerheads, green turtles, and leatherbacks. In a year, about 2,000 nests are built by mother turtles on Broward County beaches.

These turtles are protected, and there is a safe way for the public to watch nature in action. Starting in July, the Broward County Sea Turtle Conservation Program accepts reservations from the public to take part in sea turtle hatchling releases. They occur five nights a week and begin with a presentation by a sea turtle specialist at the Guy Harvey Oceanographic Center.

HATCHLING RELEASE

WHAT: An opportunity to watch baby sea turtles return to the ocean

WHERE: Guy Harvey Oceanographic Center, 8000 N Ocean Dr., Dania Beach

COST: Free to enter

PRO TIP: The releases cap at 50 people, so claim a spot as soon as you can.

Visit the Broward County Sea Turtles website to follow along with a running tally of the number and species of sea turtle nests laid in the area.

Loggerhead hatchlings emerge from their nests to make their way into the ocean. Courtesy Heiko Kiera / Shutterstock.com

Here guests will learn about the efforts made to protect sea turtles and the challenges they face, from illegal hunting to being struck by boat propellers. Then, the group will make their way to the beach as hatchlings follow the light of the moon into the Atlantic Ocean.

NINE LIVES

What's the story of Revolution Live?

Countless musical stars have taken the stage at Revolution Live when they were small fries, from Lady Gaga and Dua Lipa to 21 Pilots, Katy Perry, Jelly Roll, Post Malone, Fall Out Boy, and Arctic Monkeys, to name a few. Set up pit style, there's no bad seat at this venue that for two decades has catered to fans of all ages, genres, and eras of music.

REVOLUTION LIVE

WHAT: A concert venue and community hub that started as a slaughterhouse

WHERE: 100 SW Third Ave., Fort Lauderdale

COST: Ticket prices vary

PRO TIP: Climb up to the second-floor balcony for a unique view of the band and the crowd.

Revolution Live was founded by Jeff John in 2004; the inaugural show was The Wailers, Bob Marley's backing band. But it took more than a year of renovations to get there, as the building is more than 100 years old. It opened in 1924 as a slaughterhouse, then during World War II it was converted into an armory; with the railroad tracks running past the building, it was ideal for shipping out bullets for the war effort. Then it was the restaurant The Cajun House, the nightclub Backstreets, the concert venue The Chili Pepper, and finally, Revolution Live.

John says people constantly come up to him and share their experiences at its former iterations; it's a part of the fabric of Fort Lauderdale. Revolution Live carries the torch not only with its concerts but also by hosting community events such as Day of the Dead, Indie Craft Bazaar, and the Fort Lauderdale Food & Wine Festival. It's even been used for tactical training for local police. It was also on the silver screen (when it was converted to the Bourbon Room for *Rock of Ages*) as well as a number of television shows.

Revolution Live has been a mainstay for music in Fort Lauderdale for more than 20 years. Courtesy Geoffrey Clowes / Shutterstock.com

At the end of the day, it's about seeing people happy, John says, whether it's teenage girls screaming for a pop star or older adults singing along to their favorite band from the '80s. Rock on.

In 2018, the Pixies hosted a secret show by advertising as the band Debaser (one of its songs). Super fans and local media guessed correctly that the band had come out of retirement.

INSIDE OUT

Where did the walls of the lobby at the Parker come from?

In the main lobby of the Parker, the red carpet and Art Deco aesthetic are familiar throwbacks to what it must have looked like when it first opened back in 1967. Something else should look familiar, too, just not at its regular spot. It's the walls of the lobby as one is looking at the box office—this used to be the outside of the theatre.

The decades-old building was in need of some TLC over the years, and on the wishlist was a spacious lobby where theatergoers could congregate before shows and during intermission. However, the staff knew that the building was in the running for designation as a historical landmark. By keeping the facade but building out a lobby, the theater got the best of both worlds. The original wall, sconces, and window panes have all been refreshed. Other elements of the original building are still intact, too. On the roof, a ballerina statue has been refreshed, and inside, the mermaid statues and one of *Wizard of Oz* actress Billie Burke were moved into more prominent spaces in the lobby. In the lobby, near the restrooms, there are also placards for performers who were once inside the theater's green room: James Earl Jones, Mickey Rooney, Eartha Kitt, and Elizabeth Taylor. For Taylor, her time at the Parker was her first time performing in a play, in *The Little Foxes*.

THE PARKER

WHAT: A reimagined arts and culture center with nods to its past

WHERE: 707 NE Eighth St., Fort Lauderdale

COST: Ticket prices vary

PRO TIP: For a fee, guests of The Parker can enjoy drinks and food at The Haller Club for an hour before the show and dessert during intermission.

The Parker, originally known as the Parker Playhouse, was funded by inventor Louis Parker. He invented a device that

Above: *The exterior of The Parker includes a row of statues of the arts, such as a ballerina, author, and violinist. Photos courtesy Gonzalo Villota*

Left: *In the renovation of The Parker, the exterior became the inside box office.*

syncs up audio and video for television, and he also worked on the Apollo program. With his background in electronics and sound, it makes sense that the acoustics at the Parker are impeccable; if you stand underneath the chandeliers in the lobby, there's the perfect echo. Bravo!

The portraits of Katharine Hepburn, Yul Brynner, Phillis Diller, and other golden-age actors were painted by Louis Parker's wife.

SOURCES

One Giant Leap for Mankind

https://www.nasa.gov/missions/apollo/about-apollo-7-the-first-crewed-apollo-space-mission/

https://www.broward.org/Library/Pages/MoonRock.aspx

https://digitalarchives.broward.org/digital/collection/p16146coll10/id/736/

Desegregating the Beaches

https://www.floridastateparks.org/parks-and-trails/dr-von-d-mizell-eula-johnson-state-park/history

Swing Life Away

https://www.newspapers.com/image/230676182/?match=1&terms=swing%20bridge%20

Handle with Care

https://www.townofhillsborobeach.com/282/Barefoot-Mail-Man

https://www.newpelican.com/articles/a-restaurant-a-sculpture-and-the-boy-scouts-the-history-of-honoring-and-preserving-the-barefoot-mailman/

https://flamingomag.com/2019/09/17/floridiana-barefoot-mailman/

Collegiate Headquarters

https://www.wptv.com/sports/hockey/panthers/fort-lauderdales-elbo-room-becomes-center-of-celebration-for-florida-panthers-after-stanley-cup-win

Rest in Peace

https://www.atlasobscura.com/places/leslie-nielsen-s-gravesite-2

Aye, Aye, Captain

https://capsplace.com/history/

What a Wreck

https://shipwreckparkpompano.org/

Mythological Creatures

https://www.atlasobscura.com/places/pegasus-and-dragon

The Mystery of Flight 19

https://www.history.navy.mil/browse-by-topic/disasters-and-phenomena/flight-19.html

https://www.broward.org/Airport/Business/about/Pages/Statistics.aspx

A Farm in Fort Lauderdale

https://reginasfarm.com/

Never Forget

https://www.goriverwalk.com/9-11-monument

https://www.broward.org/Airport/passengers/Services/Pages/911Memorial.aspx

https://discoverftlbeach.com/forget-monument-lauderdale/

What's in a name?

https://fortlauderdalemagazine.com/major-lauderdales-fort/

https://www.sun-sentinel.com/1988/08/14/remembering-the-major-a-bronze-statue-of-lauderdale-on-a-horse-is-being-cast-for-new-housing-development/

A Royal Welcome

http://newspapers.com/image/228452481/?match=1&terms=countess%20lauderdale

https://www.newspapers.com/image/229873138/?match=1&terms=countess%20lauderdale

https://www.newspapers.com/image/229873526/?match=1&terms=countess%20lauderdale

https://www.newspapers.com/image/229797388/?match=1&terms=countess%20lauderdale

Tarpon and Torpedoes

https://www.lauderdalemarina.com/history

https://www.newspapers.com/image/618304227/?match=1&terms=lauderdale%20marina%20torpedo%20cox

https://www.newspapers.com/image/618304781/?match=1&terms=lauderdale%20marina%20torpedo%20cox

https://www.newpelican.com/articles/herstory-broward-countys-naval-air-station-home-base-for-a-famous-naval-mystery-also-trained-a-president/

Viktor E. for the Florida Panthers

https://www.visitflorida.com/travel-ideas/articles/sawgrass-mills-outlet-shopping-at-floridas-largest-mall/

https://www.espn.com/nhl/story/_/id/37826923/florida-panthers-fans-throw-rats-tradition-playoffs-goals

Sweet Nostalgia

http://tothemoonmarketplace.com/

https://jenis.com/collections/all-flavors

Be Kind, Rewind

https://www.sun-sentinel.com/2012/04/28/blockbuster-goes-from-boom-to-almost-bust-2/

https://www.palmbeachpost.com/story/business/2015/05/01/report-last-blockbuster-in-florida/7170186007/

https://fortlauderdaleillustrated.com/things-to-do/around-town/exhibit-honors-laudy-locals-from-long-ago/

Beam Me Up, Scotty

https://www.browardpalmbeach.com/best-of/2008/people-and-places/best-landmark-6359257

https://www.liveoaklyn.com/wp-content/uploads/2024/06/Oaklyn-Office-3101-NFH.pdf?x80625

https://fortlauderdalemagazine.com/updating-oakland-park/

https://digitalarchives.broward.org/digital/collection/bountiful/id/676/

https://www.sun-sentinel.com/2016/06/09/broward-landmark-inspired-by-a-cartoon/

https://news.google.com/newspapers?id=AadOAAAAIBAJ&sjid=QfsDAAAAIBAJ&pg=7014,5537438

https://news.google.com/newspapers?nid=888&dat=19760618&id=bMlhAAAAIBAJ&sjid=WV0DAAAAIBAJ&pg=5627,1972395

Brush with Fate

https://www.sun-sentinel.com/2003/01/19/a-brush-with-history/?share=besshnt2snrunc0hm1cs

https://backusmuseum.org/highwaymen

https://museumoffloridahistory.com/explore/collections/florida-highwaymen-collection/

A Feat of Engineering

https://fortlauderdalemagazine.com/a-boring-story/

https://www.newspapers.com/image/230458106/?match=1&terms=new%20river%20tunnel

https://en.wikipedia.org/wiki/Category:Tunnels_in_Florida

House Boat

https://www.newspapers.com/image/272584253/?match=1&terms=king-cromartie%20house

https://historyfortlauderdale.org/museum-campus

https://fortlauderdale.jl.org/about/history/

Spin Me Right Round

https://piersixtysixresidences.com/the-iconic-pier-top-lounge/

https://www.boatinternational.com/destinations/americas-yacht-destinations/fort-lauderdale-yachting-history

https://www.sun-sentinel.com/2018/07/06/6-fun-things-about-pier-66-you-probably-didnt-know/

Snow Day

https://www.cbsnews.com/miami/news/let-it-snow-let-it-snow-let-it-snow-47-years-ago-it-did-in-south-florida/

https://www.lasolasboulevard.com/christmasonlasolas

https://www.newspapers.com/image/232229153/?match=1&terms=snow%20

Monkeying Around

https://www.nbcmiami.com/news/local/all-about-animals/nonprofit-to-build-sanctuary-for-wild-monkey-colony-in-dania-beach/2633136/

https://vervetproject.org/history-of-the-dania-beach-monkeys/

Hunting Grounds

https://flpythonchallenge.org/participate/competition/winners/

https://flpythonchallenge.org/participate/competition/rules/

https://myfwc.com/wildlifehabitats/profiles/reptiles/snakes/burmese-python/

https://www.nps.gov/ever/learn/nature/burmese-python.htm#:~:text=Burmese%20pythons%20are%20established%20in,number%20in%20Everglades%20National%20Park

https://www.miamiherald.com/news/local/environment/article283594748.html

https://www.palmbeachpost.com/story/entertainment/2025/01/02/florida-alligator-tows-colossal-python-through-everglades-water-video/76864251007/

Beware of Whirlpools

https://www.newspapers.com/image/230241368/?match=1&terms=whirlpool%20new%20river

https://www.browardpalmbeach.com/news/wild-and-dirty-6317587

https://www.facebook.com/LegendsLoreNewRiver/posts/one-of-the-fascinating-early-mysteries-of-fort-lauderdales-new-river-was-at-leas/433204992037541/

http://newspapers.com/image/271778038/?match=1&terms=whirlpool%20river

https://www.newspapers.com/image/232946189/?match=1&terms=whirlpool%20lola

Splendid Sea Cows

https://www.sunrisepaddleboards.com/manatee-fort-lauderdale/

https://www.porteverglades.net/environment/manatee-season/

https://www.broward.org/Manatees/Pages/Default.aspx

https://apps.apple.com/us/app/i-spy-a-manatee/id1313288109

https://myfwc.com/education/wildlife/manatee/facts-and-information/

https://www.fpl.com/clean-energy/natural-gas/port-everglades.html

Blow Me Away

https://hollywoodfl.org/Facilities/Facility/Details/ArtsPark-at-Young-Circle-87

https://www.hollywoodhotglass.com/hot-glass-class.html

Telling Time

https://mods.org/exhibit/great-gravity-clock/

https://www.sun-sentinel.com/2017/04/04/mods-great-gravity-clock-is-back-just-in-time/

Tiny Town

https://www.sunrisefl.gov/Home/Components/FacilityDirectory/FacilityDirectory/42/258?npage=2

Lady of the House

https://www.bonnethouse.org/about-all/

https://www.bonnethouse.org/history/

https://www.bonnethouse.org/art/

It's a Bird, It's a Plane, It's a Blimp

https://visitpompano.com/see-do/goodyear-blimp-base/

https://www.smithsonianmag.com/smart-news/a-brief-history-of-the-goodyear-blimp-which-celebrates-its-100th-anniversary-this-year-180985772/

https://www.goodyear.com/en_US/blimp.html

https://www.goodyear.com/en_US/blimp/information/current-blimps.html

Odds and Ends

https://www.instagram.com/oddballsniftythrift/?hl=en

https://blog.yelp.com/community/the-top-vintage-and-consignment-shops-in-the-usa/

A Legacy of Change

https://stonewall-museum.org/

https://www.visitlauderdale.com/articles/post/the-evolution-and-significance-of-the-lgbt-community-in-fort-lauderdale/

https://www.sun-sentinel.com/2012/06/27/dont-ask-dont-tell-gavel-unlikely-to-head-to-washington/

A Treasure Trove of Black History

https://broward.lyrasistechnology.org/repositories/2/resources?

https://www.broward.org/Library/Events/SoFloBookFest/pages/default.aspx

A Scoop For Me, a Scoop For You

https://www.jaxsonsicecream.com/

Open Sesame

https://www.roomnine01.com/

https://www.wlrn.org/whats-the-story/2014-12-02/broward-countys-watery-relationship-with-the-everglades-over-a-century

https://fortlauderdalemagazine.com/the-tale-of-fort-liquordale/

It's Just a Party, Janet

https://www.fandango.com/paradigm-cinemas-gateway-fort-lauderdale-aaggt/theater-page?format=all

https://fortlauderdalemagazine.com/gateway-at-the-crossroads/

https://www.facebook.com/TheGatewayCinema/paradigmcinemas.com

The Story of Rubin Stacy

https://www.newspapers.com/image/230160949/?match=1&terms=lynching

https://www.cbsnews.com/miami/news/rubin-stacy-memorial-boulevard-renaming/

Painting Reality

https://collection.nsuartmuseum.org/mwebcgi/mweb.exe?request=record;id=16283;type=101

https://www.pbs.org/weta/fridakahlo/resources/locations.html

https://nsuartmuseum.org/exhibition/kahlo-rivera-mexican-modern-art/

https://collection.nsuartmuseum.org/mwebcgi/mweb.exe?request=record;id=228;type=901

Something Fishy

https://www.visitpompanobeach.com/things-to-do/beach/

https://www.pompanobeachfl.gov/government/cra/cra-projects/pier-development

https://parks.pompanobeachfl.gov/parks-beach-and-pier/fisher-family-pier

https://venicemagftl.com/pier-to-pier/

Book Worms

https://www.oldfloridabookshop.com/

167 Steps to the Top

https://www.hillsborolighthouse.org/

Pssst Pssst Pssst

https://ladyluckanimalrescue.com/cat-cafe/

https://www.newpelican.com/articles/a-kitty-with-your-coffee/

O, Christmas Tree

https://thechristmaspalace.com/

Cultural Reunion

https://semtribefair.com/about-tribal-fair/

Cowboy Town

https://www.floridabeef.org/raising-beef/cattle-in-florida

https://davieprorodeo.com/dpr/

https://10best.usatoday.com/awards/travel/best-rodeo-2024/

Go With The Flo

https://thefloridiandiner.com/

https://www.sun-sentinel.com/2023/04/25/butch-samp-owner-of-the-floridian-diner-in-fort-lauderdale-dies/

High Dive

https://venicemagftl.com/in-retrospect-international-swimming-hall-of-fame/

https://www.parks.fortlauderdale.gov/beach/aquatics/fort-lauderdale-aquatic-complex/history-world-records

https://www.swimmingworldmagazine.com/news/city-of-fort-lauderdale-opened-the-las-olas-casino-pool-93-years-ago-today/

Mount Trashmore

https://www.cbsnews.com/miami/news/hollywood-comes-to-south-florida/

https://www.wmsolutions.com/locations/details/id/127

On the Shoulders of Giants

https://discoverftlbeach.com/things-to-do/dc-alexander-park/

Stargazing

https://www.sfaaa.com/#about

https://markhampark.com/the-fox-observatory/

Choo, Choo

https://livesteamers.org/schedule

https://www.broward.org/Parks/ThingsToDo/Pages/SteamTrainRides.aspx

From Rum Runners to Kayakers

https://www.newspapers.com/image/236082620/?match=1&terms=whiskey%20creek

https://whiskeycreekhideout.com/about-us/

https://www.newspapers.com/image/272332137/?match=1&terms=whiskey%20creek

https://www.foxnews.com/lifestyle/this-day-history-october-29-1964-gems-stolen-jewel-heist-century

Venice of America

https://www.lasolasgondola.com/gondola-tours/

https://www.facebook.com/LasOlasGondolaRide

Remember Me

https://www.dayofthedeadflorida.com/

https://kids.nationalgeographic.com/celebrations/article/day-of-the-dead

https://www.sun-sentinel.com/2023/10/27/how-day-of-the-dead-in-fort-lauderdale-almost-didnt-happen/

Float Like a Butterfly

https://butterflyworld.com/

Give Me Liberty or Give Me Death

https://america250pa.org/PPE:_Liberty_Trees

https://www.militarydisneytips.com/blog/patriotic-disney/walt-disney-worlds-liberty-tree/

https://www.newspapers.com/image/232141676/?match=1&terms=bicentennial%20tree

https://www.newspapers.com/image/231746988/?match=1&terms=live%20oak%20tree

Sandy Holidays

https://discoverftlbeach.com/happy-holidays-from-ftlbeach/

https://discoverftlbeach.com/event/light-up-the-beach/

A Rockin' Light Show

https://casino.hardrock.com/hollywood/hotel/the-guitar-hotel

Dinner and a Show

https://junglequeen.com/about-us-jungle-queen-cruising-since-1935/

Animal Kingdom

https://outsfl.com/wilton-manors/wilton-manors-holds-ceremony-to-welcome-thunderbunny-to-the-drive

https://www.prnewswire.com/news-releases/city-of-wilton-manors-to-host-ribbon-cutting-ceremony-for-thunderbunny-public-art-installation-302030145.html

https://www.facebook.com/photo/?fbid=5940274582755269&set=a.110391755743610

https://www.facebook.com/photo?fbid=390891353571778&set=a.157501846910731

https://www.inplainsightwm.com/

Under the Sea

https://www.boceanresort.com/mermaids-at-the-wreck-bar/#none

https://www.boceanresort.com/mermaid-shows-at-the-wreck-bar/

https://fortlauderdalemagazine.com/yankee-pride/

A Student of History

https://www.browardschools.com/Page/35769

https://venicemagftl.com/in-retrospect-lucky-number-eleven/

Like Mother, Like Daughter

https://www.mymamasdania.com/

No Limit

https://www.yeswearemadarts.com/

Bathing Beauties

https://www.broward.org/History/NationalRegister/Pages/CroissantParkAdministrationBuilding.aspx

https://npgallery.nps.gov/GetAsset/ad328c9c-2355-486a-a965-2c1ea92f2575

https://cflca.org/croissant-park/

https://www.newspapers.com/image/228444861/?match=1&terms=croissant%20park

https://www.newspapers.com/image/228446308/?match=1&terms=croissant%20park%20bathing%20beauties

https://www.newspapers.com/image/228444089/?match=1&terms=bathing%20beauty%20croissant%20park

https://www.newspapers.com/image/228447610/?match=1&terms=miss%20lauderdale

Lights, Camera, Action

https://www.local10.com/sports/2020/07/24/caddyshack-turns-40-heres-where-they-filmed-it-in-south-florida/

https://fortlauderdalemagazine.com/as-seen-on-the-screen/

https://www.browardpalmbeach.com/news/top-ten-films-shot-in-fort-lauderdale-6460380

https://en.wikipedia.org/wiki/The_Idol_Dancer#/media/File:The_Idol_Dancer_-_Lobby_card_-_A_-_1920.jpg

Welcome, Mr. President

https://www.facebook.com/ftlhistory/photos/welcoming-president-elect-warren-g-harding-in-1921top-looking-south-andrews-ave-/10159626920369850/

https://www.palmbeachdailynews.com/picture-gallery/news/history/2021/03/08/photos-president-harding-made-visits-palm-beach/4628769001/

https://www.floridamemory.com/items/show/274304

Just Breathe

https://danielpopper.com/work/thrive/

Governor Broward

https://dos.fl.gov/florida-facts/florida-history/florida-governors/napoleon-bonaparte-broward/

https://www.nga.org/governor/napoleon-bonaparte-broward/

https://www.sfwmd.gov/sites/default/files/documents/panel1-5.pdf

http://www.floridahistorynetwork.com/april-30-1915---broward-county-created-named-after-former-governor.html

https://apnews.com/general-news-e1853fdef19f4b24824d8de407799539

https://www.wlrn.org/news/2017-10-20/gov-browards-family-speaks-up-after-his-statue-was-removed-from-courthouse

https://ufdc.ufl.edu/UF00102917/00002

https://www.sun-sentinel.com/2017/10/19/family-says-theres-more-to-gov-broward-than-just-one-speech/

It's a Jungle Out There

https://www.sun-sentinel.com/2002/04/12/long-ago-in-lauderdale/

https://archive.org/details/62824CastleFilmsClydeBeattysAnimalThrills

https://venicemagftl.com/in-retrospect-feature-films/

https://www.bonnethouse.org/wp-content/uploads/2017/03/Apr June-2014-Newsletter-Compressed.pdf

https://flamingogardens.org/wildlife-sanctuary/

https://www.findagrave.com/memorial/135610894/harriett-beatty

See You Later, Alligator

https://www.newspapers.com/image/718529160/?match=1&terms=elvis%20alligator

https://www.sun-sentinel.com/1990/09/22/a-finer-flamingo-some-say-flamingo-gardens-lost-more-than-its-roadside-gator-zoo-in-may-some-say-the-27-year-old-davie-attraction-has-lost-its-soul/

https://www.sun-sentinel.com/1985/10/02/davie-alligator-makes-good-in-role-as-sonnys-scaly-pal-in-miami-vice/

Holly Jolly Ahoy

https://winterfestparade.com/

For Whom the Bell Tolls

https://stranahanhouse.org/history/

See Your Gypsy

https://www.sun-sentinel.com/1986/04/20/digging-with-gypsy-graves-she-works-in-tombs-and-befriends-the-dead-welcome-to-the-south-florida-of-3000-bc/

https://www.browardpalmbeach.com/news/raze-the-roof-6327513

https://www.sun-sentinel.com/1990/10/14/the-past-seeks-a-home-in-fort-lauderdale/

https://www.iviefuneralhome.com/obituaries/Gypsy-Graves?obId=20521413

https://www.sun-sentinel.com/2004/07/24/graves-museum-shut-future-uncertain/

Burger Joint

http://instagram.com/p/CEkI5txBWo4/

https://www.jacksoldfashionburgers.com/

https://www.legacy.com/us/obituaries/sunsentinel/name/jack-berry-obituary?id=6838543

https://www.palmbeachpost.com/story/news/crime/2011/02/12/jack-berry-founder-jack-s/7156887007/

https://www.sun-sentinel.com/2006/05/05/jacks-old-fashion-hamburger-housefort-lauderdale/

Pop Culture Fandom

https://tatescomics.com/

Seminole Girl

https://seminoletribune.org/seminole-girl-at-home-on-new-river/

https://seminoletribune.org/seminole-girl-returns-to-fort-lauderdale-site/

https://www.sun-sentinel.com/2023/01/24/fort-lauderdales-seminole-girl-statue-has-gone-missing-dont-worry-it-wasnt-stolen/

https://fortlauderdalemagazine.com/mother-lauderdale/

Turtle Power

https://hcas.nova.edu/seaturtles/

https://www.broward.org/NaturalResources/BeachAndMarine/SeaTurtles/Pages/default.aspx

https://www.facebook.com/browardcturtles/events

Nine Lives

https://www.jointherevolution.net/

Inside Out

https://www.newpelican.com/articles/the-parker-reimagining-and-revamping-a-fort-lauderdale-landmark/

https://www.sun-sentinel.com/1993/06/22/donor-of-parker-playhouse-dies/

https://playbill.com/article/read-playbills-interview-with-elizabeth-taylor-upon-her-broadway-debut

INDEX

DR LUBE
E31447
2 NUTS
FAMOUS
MS DISH
M00000
LATELY
NO PIGS
RANDOM
BARK WND
Ye Old Johns
STINK
546 AK
OHIO
QUEBEC
4K-3075
SHAMPOO
TONTO
ONE TON
MIKE
JANICE
OH YEAH
DR-28
EMERGENCY
TELEPHONE
LKY STAR
RB 4570
A-20
GZ · 48
HZ · 8
1721
1920
2 SHARPE
MMMN
3912W
MRS-POO
MR-POO
MONGO3
MOHEL-1
N-MASON
W. 36
7TH AVE.
UDELL ST
LINDA
HAIRKT
BUDEE
NEW JERSEY
LOVE
401HWY
VH78
REST

STAR WARS
AHSOKA
SCULPTURE
COLIN CHRISTIAN
Trivial Pursuit
STAR WARS
PLEASE
DO NOT UCH
POR FAVOR
NO TOCAR